THE

GOSPEL OF

MARK:

DISPENSATIONALLY CONSIDERED

A GRACE EXPOSITIONAL COMMENTARY

Dr. David Alan Greene

GraceWord Publishing, LLC
www.gracewordpublishing.com
U.S.A.

GRACEWORD PUBLISHING

Contents

To B'nai Avraham — the children of Abraham

Now I say that
Jesus Christ
was a minister of the circumcision
for the truth of God,
to confirm the promises
made unto the fathers:

– The Apostle Paul

x

Acknowledgements

I would like to express a special thanks to Jon and Susan McMahon and Frances Greene for their continued encouragement. To those who assisted with the preparation of this book, I offer my gratitude.

Introduction

Dear reader if you have read some of my other commentaries on the gospels, you will note that the Introductions are very similar. The introduction plays a key role in understanding the material presented. The reader should be familiar with the concept and application of rightly dividing the Word of Truth. It is also known as the dispensational approach to Scripture. When God ordered the Bible, He divided it into ages or dispensations. Each of these divisions were intended to lead towards His ultimate goal of restoring His Creation.

Traditionally, the Bible has been divided into seven ages or periods of time. Sometimes, these divisions are referred to as administrations in which God chose to make Himself known. There is a progression in these administrations which leads to its conclusion. Jumping into the middle of a book or movie series does not allow the reader to fully understand or enjoy the series in full.

GraceWord Publishing has created the Grace Expositional Bible Commentary. Each of the books included in the series walks the reader through the biblical book verse-by-verse. As this is done, it applies a system or method of interpretation. For this reason, I recommend the reader be familiar with the simple concept of "rightly dividing" the Word of Truth. Paul instructed his student, Timothy, in 2 Timothy 2:15:

> 15 **Study to shew thyself approved unto God, a workman that needeth not to be ashamed, <u>rightly dividing the word of truth</u>.**

For us to understand any portion of Scripture, we must see it within its proper division. It is dangerous to take verses of Scripture out of its context. Doing so will increase the risk of missing the point entirely or misunderstanding to whom the text was intended.

Like the number of days that God took to create the earth, I believe there are seven periods of time or ages or dispensations that He will take to redeem His Creation. The Gospel of Matthew opens in the middle of the fifth dispensation which is the Age of Law. The Jews received the Law from Moses after God used him to lead His people out of Egypt. It was in the Wilderness that God created Israel to be a "peculiar" or special people — a holy nation separated from all the other nations. Israel has a purpose!

God told Moses to speak to Israel. Exodus 19:6:

> 6 And <u>ye shall be unto me a kingdom of priests, and an holy nation</u>. These are the words which thou shalt speak unto the children of Israel.

This is God's ultimate purpose for Israel. They will play a key role in His restored Creation.

Mosaic Covenant

Through Moses, God offered the children of Abraham, Isaac, and Jacob a binding contract or covenant. It would contractually bind God and His people. In the verses that follow, notice the offer and the acceptance. The people bound themselves to this conditional agreement. Verses 7-8:

> 7 And Moses came and called for the elders of the people, and laid before their faces all these words which the LORD commanded him.
>
> 8 <u>And all the people answered together, and said, All that the LORD hath spo-</u>

ken we will do. And Moses returned the words of the people unto the LORD.

This agreement or covenant remains in effect even to this day. This fact is important. Nothing has changed for the Jews since the day they voluntarily accepted the terms of this agreement. God has not voided this covenant in spite of Israel's actions.

This means that the Law remained in full effect throughout Jesus' earthly ministry. Consider His words in the Sermon of the Mount. A multitude of Jews gathered to hear Him speak. Matthew 5:17-18:

> 17 **Think not that I am come to destroy the law, or the prophets: I am not come to destroy, but to fulfil.**
>
> 18 **For verily I say unto you, Till heaven and earth pass, one jot or one tittle shall in no wise pass from the law, till [until it] all be fulfilled.**

So, the Law will be fulfilled at the end of the restoration. Jesus Christ is the One Who fulfills the Law.

Even after His death and resurrection, those who follow his Gospel of the Kingdom remain bound to the Law. Much later in the book of James, the Apostle James wrote to the children of Abraham as they await the return of their Messiah. Look how he addresses his letter which was sent to comfort and encourage the Kingdom Believers. James 1:1:

> 1 **James, a servant of God and of the Lord Jesus Christ, <u>to the twelve tribes which are scattered abroad, greeting</u>.**

Knowing to whom James wrote this letter reveals something important. It becomes clear that the Law is still in effect for the Jews who follow the Gospel of the Kingdom. James, who was one of the Twelve, wrote this in verse 2:10:

> 10 **For whosoever shall keep the whole law, and yet offend [break] in one point, he is guilty of all.**

James is not telling them but reminding them of their obligation according to the Mosaic Covenant. The entire Law was read aloud to those in the Wilderness as it is read to the congregation every year. Let us look at this again. Exodus 19:8:

> 8 **And all the people answered together, and said, <u>All that the LORD hath spoken we will do</u>. And Moses returned the words of the people unto the LORD.**

Notice it is not "some" of what God said, but "all" that God said. The first five books of the Bible are called the "books of Moses." In the fifth book, Deuteronomy, there is a portion of the Mosaic Covenant which is referred to as the "blessings and curses." For this, it is clear that this covenant is conditional. If they obey and do what is right according to the covenant, God will bless them. However, if they break one point of the covenant, God will curse or punish them. James reiterated this point in his letter to them. He reminds them of their commitment to this lasting covenant.

Evidence speaks louder that opinion. Here are two portions from Deuteronomy 28. The first portion is referred to as "the blessings." Verses 1-2:

> 1 **And it shall come to pass, if thou shalt hearken diligently unto the voice of the LORD thy God, <u>to observe and to do all his commandments which I command thee this day</u>, that the LORD thy God will set thee on high above all nations of the earth:**

> 2 **And all these blessings shall come on thee, and overtake thee, if thou shalt hearken unto the voice of the LORD thy God.**

The second portion is referred to as "the curses." These are the consequences for failure to keep the Law in its entirety. Verse 15:

> 15 But it shall come to pass, if thou wilt not hearken unto the voice of the LORD thy God, <u>to observe to do all his commandments and his statutes which I command thee this day;</u> that all these curses shall come upon thee, and overtake thee:

The word "all" plays a critical part in God's expectations of the children of Abraham, Isaac, and Israel.

From Moses, King David, his son King Solomon, and all the Old Testament prophets, the Law of Moses was in effect. Nothing had changed when Jesus was born. Later, the Apostle Paul explains that <u>Jesus was under the Law</u> and <u>He came to redeem those who were under the Law</u>. Galatians 4:4-5:

> 4 But when the fulness of the time was come, God sent forth his Son, made of a woman, <u>made under the law,</u> 5 <u>To redeem them that were under the law,</u> that we might receive the adoption of sons.

There are two other covenants in the Old Testament that will have an impact on the people in the Gospel of Mark. In addition to the Mosaic Covenant, other covenants were made with Abraham and King David. The Jews were taught well and they knew their Scripture. It gave them hope for the future because they trusted that God would fulfill them. Both of these are unconditional which means that God will fulfill these covenants regardless of Israel's actions. Here, they are summarized:

Abrahamic Covenant:

The following is found in Genesis 12:1-3:

1 **Now the LORD had said unto Abram, Get thee out of thy country, and from thy kindred, and from thy father's house, unto a land that I will shew thee:**

2 **And I will make of thee a great nation, and I will bless thee, and make thy name great; and thou shalt be a blessing:**

3 **And I will bless them that bless thee, and curse him that curseth thee: and in thee shall all families of the earth be blessed.**

Davidic Covenant:

God told the prophet Nathan to deliver this message to King David. 2 Samuel 7:12-13:

> 12 **And when thy days be fulfilled, and thou shalt sleep with thy fathers, <u>I will set up thy seed after thee</u>, which shall proceed out of thy bowels, <u>and I will establish his kingdom</u>.**

> 13 **He shall build an house for my name, and <u>I will stablish the throne of his kingdom for ever</u>.**

The Seed or Son of David will be Jesus Christ. Verses 14-16:

> 14 **I will be his father, and he shall be my son. If he commit iniquity, I will chasten him with the rod of men, and with the stripes of the children of men: 15 But my mercy shall not depart away from him, as I took it from Saul, whom I put away before thee.**

> 16 **And thine house and thy kingdom shall be established for ever before thee: thy throne shall be established for**

ever.

I believe knowing these facts adds a deeper understanding of the Word of Truth. For the more advanced student, you may wish to consider reading *Letters To Theophilus: Are You Ready For The End Times?* and *The Glorious Destiny of Israel: The Fulfillment of God's Promises and Prophecies to Israel.* These two books present "two sides of the same coin" from the perspective of both the non-Jew and Jew respectively. Others may enjoy reading an overall summary of the Bible found in *The Hidden Gospel: Once Hidden But Now Revealed.* It highlights key events in the Bible and explains how it all comes together in the end. Some are available on audiobooks.

It is my hope that people will learn, understand, and enjoy their Bible.

1

About the Apostle Mark

Mark the Evangelist was one of four men who wrote the books known as "the gospels." The Gospel of Mark is the second of the three synoptic gospels. These are the historical records of Jesus' earthly ministry including accounts of His life, teachings, and miracles. The synoptic gospels can be placed side by side which makes for easy comparison of their content. Concerning the gospels, many theologians believe that the Gospel of Mark was written first. It may have provided an example in which the others followed. The Apostle Mark was not one of the original disciples as we see from the list of disciples named by Jesus in Matthew 10:2-4:

> 2 Now the names of the twelve apostles are these; The first, Simon, who is called Peter, and Andrew his brother; James the son of Zebedee, and John his

brother; 3 Philip, and Bartholomew; Thomas, and Matthew the publican; James the son of Alphaeus, and Lebbaeus, whose surname was Thaddaeus; 4 Simon the Canaanite, and Judas Iscariot, who also betrayed him.

Although Mark was not one of the original Twelve, he was one of the early believers. He remained close to the Apostle Peter who named him in the salutation of his first epistle calling him "Marcus my son"(1 Pet. 5:13). In the same manner in which Paul referred to Timothy as his "son in the faith" (1 Tim. 1:2). It is clear that Peter had a close relationship with Mark and an impact on his training.

When Peter escaped from Herod's prison, he went to the home of Marks' mother. Acts 12:11-12:

11 And when Peter was come to himself, he said, Now I know of a surety, that the Lord hath sent his angel, and hath delivered me out of the hand of Herod, and from all the expectation of the people of the Jews.

12 And when he had considered the thing, he came to the house of Mary the mother of John, whose surname was

Mark; where many were gathered together praying.

It was her home where the believers had gathered to pray. Later, Mark traveled with the Apostle Paul and Barnabas during their first missionary journey. However, Mark did not continue on this journey but chose to return home. This created a problem for Paul who had a highly driven temperament. Acts 15:36-40:

> 36 And some days after Paul said unto Barnabas, Let us go again and visit our brethren in every city where we have preached the word of the Lord, and see how they do.
>
> 37 And Barnabas determined to take with them John, whose surname was Mark. 38 But Paul thought not good to take him with them, who departed from them from Pamphylia, and went not with them to the work.
>
> 39 And the contention was so sharp between them, that they departed asunder one from the other: and so Barnabas took Mark, and sailed unto Cyprus;

40 **And Paul chose Silas, and departed, being recommended by the brethren unto the grace of God.**

This argument may have been due to Mark's passive temperament which was not conducive to Paul's mission. However, "... we know that all things work together for good to them that love God, to them who are the called according to his purpose" (Rom. 8:28). As a result of this disagreement, there were two separate missionary teams sent instead of one.

Although Paul and Mark parted company, his love for Paul during his imprisonment in Rome shows his continued devotion to the saints. During his imprisonment in Rome, Paul wrote his last letter to Timothy. In it, he mentions that all have left him except Luke. He mentions Mark and his usefulness to him in the ministry. 2 Timothy 4:11

11 **Only Luke is with me. <u>Take Mark, and bring him with thee: for he is profitable to me for the ministry</u>.**

Later, Paul mentions Mark in his letter to the believers in Colosse endorsing him to them. In this, we find that Mark is the son of Barnabas' sister. Colossians 4:10:

10 Aristarchus my fellowprisoner saluteth you, <u>and Marcus, sister's son to Barnabas,</u> (touching whom ye received commandments: if he come unto you, receive him;)

There are few biblical references concerning Mark's ministry or death. The historian Eusebius recorded some facts about the Apostle Mark which provide a background on his gospel. Eusebius states that Mark acted as a scribe for the Apostle Peter often acting as his interpreter. He kept notes on his teaching. Mark eventually arranged these sayings into his gospel. Therefore, it was the recollections of Peter who was an eyewitness that lead to the creation of the Gospel of Mark. According to church history, the Apostle Mark was martyred between 68 and 74 A.D.

2

Mark 1

Mark's gospel begins with the prophecy concerning John the Baptist as a voice "crying in the wilderness." This "crying out" was proclaiming the arrival of the promised Messiah. Mark 1:1-3:

> **1 The beginning of the gospel of Jesus Christ [Messiah], the Son of God; 2 As it is written in the prophets, Behold, I send my messenger before thy face, which shall prepare thy way before thee.**
>
> **3 The voice of one crying in the wilderness, Prepare ye the way of the Lord, make his paths straight.**

Fulfillment of prophecy assures us of God's faithfulness of His Word. Let us take a look at this prophecy in Isaiah 40:3-5:

> 3 The voice of him that crieth in the wilderness, Prepare ye the way of the LORD, make straight in the desert a highway for our God.
>
> 4 Every valley shall be exalted, and every mountain and hill shall be made low: and the crooked shall be made straight, and the rough places plain:
>
> 5 **And the glory of the LORD shall be revealed, and all flesh shall see it together: for the mouth of the LORD hath spoken it.**

Mark explains that what God had spoken was now coming to pass. Mark 1:4-8:

> 4 John did baptize in the wilderness, and preach <u>the baptism of repentance for the remission of sins.</u>
>
> 5 And there went out unto him all the land of Judaea, and they of Jerusalem, and were all baptized of [by] him in the river of Jordan, confessing their sins.

6 And John was clothed with camel's hair, and with a girdle of a skin about his loins; and he did eat locusts and wild honey;

7 And preached, saying, There cometh one mightier than I after me, the latchet of whose shoes I am not worthy to stoop down and unloose. 8 I indeed have baptized you with water: but he shall baptize you with the Holy Ghost.

Mark moves directly to Jesus' baptism by John the Baptist. Verses 9-11:

9 And it came to pass in those days, that Jesus came from Nazareth of Galilee, and was baptized of John in Jordan.

10 And straightway coming up out of the water, he saw the heavens opened, and the Spirit like a dove descending upon him:

11 And there came a voice from heaven, saying, <u>Thou art my beloved Son, in whom I am well pleased.</u>

Many who are led by the Spirit often feel compelled

to do something. This was the case with Jesus Who was led by the Spirit into the Wilderness in order to be tested. Verses 12-13:

> 12 **And immediately the Spirit driveth him into the wilderness.**
>
> 13 **And he was there in the wilderness forty days, tempted of Satan; and was with the wild beasts; and the angels ministered unto him.**

Mark chose not to record the details of Jesus' testing as does Matthew and Luke. (See Matthew 4:1-11 and Luke 4:1-15.)

Mark records the beginning of Jesus' ministry. Verses 14-15:

> 14 **Now after that John was put in prison, Jesus came into Galilee, preaching <u>the gospel of the kingdom</u> of God,**
>
> 15 **And saying, The time is fulfilled, and <u>the kingdom of God</u> is at hand: repent ye, and believe the gospel.**

He begins by selecting those men who would accompany Him throughout His ministry. Verses 16-20:

16 Now as he walked by the sea of Galilee, he saw Simon [Peter] and Andrew his brother casting a net into the sea: for they were fishers.

17 And Jesus said unto them, Come ye after me, and I will make you to become fishers of men. 18 And straightway they forsook their nets, and followed him.

19 And when he had gone a little further thence, he saw James the son of Zebedee, and John his brother, who also were in the ship mending their nets. 20 And straightway he called them: and they left their father Zebedee in the ship with the hired servants, and went after him.

Jesus began to teach in the synagogue which is a place of worship and religious instruction in the Jewish faith. Scribes would normally be the ones who taught the people from the Law, Prophets, and Writings, but Jesus was different. Verses 21-22:

21 And they went into Capernaum; and straightway on the sabbath day he entered into the synagogue, and taught.

22 And they were astonished at his doctrine: for he taught them as one that had authority, and not as the scribes.

The Messiah would be credentialed by God by miracles, signs, and wonders. These would be the proof the Jews needed to believe God's messenger. A circumstance presented itself while He was in the synagogue. An "unclean" spirit would be one of a demonic nature. Verses 23-27:

23 And there was in their synagogue a man with an unclean spirit; and he cried out,

24 Saying, Let us alone; what have we to do with thee, thou Jesus of Nazareth? art thou come to destroy us? I know thee who thou art, <u>the Holy One of God</u>.

25 And Jesus rebuked him, saying, Hold thy peace, and come out of him. 26 And when the unclean spirit had torn him, and cried with a loud voice, he came out of him.

27 And they were all amazed, insomuch that they questioned among themselves, saying, What thing is this? what

new doctrine is this? for with authority commandeth he even the unclean spirits, and they do obey him.

The news of this supernatural event spread quickly by word of mouth as we will see shortly. Verse 28:

28 **And immediately his fame spread abroad throughout all the region round about Galilee.**

Jesus and His disciples walked to a neighboring home. There, He performed a healing. Verses 29-31:

29 **And forthwith, when they were come out of the synagogue, they entered into the house of Simon and Andrew, with James and John.**

30 **But Simon's wife's mother lay sick of a fever, and anon [directly] they tell him of her.**

31 **And he came and took her by the hand, and lifted her up; and immediately the fever left her, and she ministered unto them.**

This is the beginning of His fame as it spread throughout the area. Verses 32-34:

> 32 And at even, when the sun did set, they brought unto him all that were diseased, and them that were possessed with devils [demons]. 33 And all the city was gathered together at the door.

> 34 And he healed many that were sick of divers diseases, and cast out many devils; and suffered not the devils to speak, because they knew him.

Jesus needed time with His Father where He could discuss the events of the day. Many of us with busy lives should take the time to check in daily with our heavenly Father. Verse 35:

> 35 And in the morning, rising up a great while before day, he went out, and departed into a solitary place, and there prayed.

His disciples noticed Him leaving and followed after Him. Verses 36-38:

> 36 And Simon and they that were with him followed after him. 37 And when

they had found him, they said unto him, All men seek for thee.

38 And he said unto them, Let us go into the next towns, that I may preach there also: for therefore [this reason] came I forth.

Galilee is located in the northern part of Israel near where modern-day Syria, Lebanon, and Jordan meet. This area includes the Sea of Galilee which is a large freshwater lake located approximately 700 feet below sea level. It is the lowest fresh water lake in the world. It has an approximate length of thirteen miles, width of eight miles, and a depth of 141 feet at its deepest point. Jesus would spend much of His early ministry here. Verses 39-44:

39 And he preached in their synagogues throughout all Galilee, and cast out devils [demons].

40 And there came a leper to him, beseeching him, and kneeling down to him, and saying unto him, If thou wilt [desires], thou canst make me clean.

41 And Jesus, moved with compassion, put forth his hand, and touched him,

and saith unto him, I will; be thou clean. 42 And as soon as he had spoken, immediately the leprosy departed from him, and he was cleansed.

43 And he [Jesus] straitly charged him, and forthwith sent him away; 44 And saith unto him, See thou say nothing to any man: but go thy way, shew thyself to the priest, and offer for thy cleansing those things which Moses commanded, for a testimony unto them.

Jesus knew that His instructions to this man would be ignored. He knew what the result of His increased notoriety would be. He would eventually need to teach outside the cities. Verse 45:

45 But he [the man] went out, and began to publish it much, and to blaze abroad the matter, insomuch that Jesus could no more openly enter into the city, but was without [outside] in desert places: and they came to him from every quarter.

3

Mark 2

Capernaum is situated on the northwest shore of the Sea of Galilee. Jesus traveled there with His disciples. Mark 2:1-2:

> 1 **And again he entered into Capernaum after some days; and it was noised [made known] that he was in the house.**
>
> 2 **And straightway [immediately] many were gathered together, insomuch that there was no room to receive them, no, not so much as about the door: and he preached the word unto them.**

Many were desperate for healing of their afflictions and brought those in need to Him. Verses 3-5:

> 3 **And they come unto him, bringing**

one sick of the palsy, which was borne of four.

4 And when they could not come nigh [near] unto him for the press [crowd], they uncovered the roof where he was: and when they had broken it up, they let down the bed wherein the sick of the palsy lay.

5 When Jesus saw their faith, he said unto the sick of the palsy, Son, thy sins be forgiven thee.

Scribes are those who are trained in the Law of Moses. They had heard the rumors and had come to see for themselves. Verses 6-12:

6 But there were certain of the scribes sitting there, and reasoning in their hearts, 7 Why doth this man thus speak blasphemies? who can forgive sins but God only?

8 And immediately when Jesus perceived in his spirit that they so reasoned within themselves, he said unto them, Why reason ye these things in your hearts?

9 Whether is it easier to say to the sick of the palsy, Thy sins be forgiven thee; or to say, Arise, and take up thy bed, and walk?

10 But that ye may know that <u>the Son of man hath power on earth to forgive sins,</u> (he saith to the sick of the palsy,)

11 I say unto thee, Arise, and take up thy bed, and go thy way into thine house. 12 And immediately he arose, took up the bed, and went forth before them all; insomuch that they were all amazed, and glorified God, saying, We never saw it on this fashion [like this].

He moved to an area outside the city along the sea. And, on His way, he saw Matthew whose name in Hebrew is Levi. Verses 13-14:

13 And he went forth again by the sea side; and all the multitude resorted [went] unto him, and he taught them.

14 And as he passed by, he saw Levi the son of Alphaeus sitting at the receipt of custom, and said unto him, Follow me. And he arose and followed him.

Matthew was a tax collector and it appears that he prepared a meal for Jesus, His disciples, and other publicans or fellow tax collectors. Verse 15-16:

> 15 And it came to pass, that, as Jesus sat at meat [meal] in his [Matthew's] house, many publicans and sinners sat also together with Jesus and his disciples: for there were many, and they followed him.

> 16 And when the scribes and Pharisees saw him eat with publicans and sinners, they said unto his disciples, How is it that he eateth and drinketh with publicans and sinners?

The Pharisees and their scribes were leaders over Israel. They taught and administered the Mosaic Law and the Levitical priesthood. They considered themselves the authorities and examples of righteousness. Verse 17:

> 17 When Jesus heard it, he saith unto them, They that are whole have no need of the physician, but they that are sick: I came not to call the righteous, but sinners to repentance.

John the Baptist had disciples who followed John much like Jesus' disciples followed Him. They came to see Jesus. Verses 18-20:

18 And the disciples of John and of the Pharisees used to fast: and they come and say unto him, Why do the disciples of John and of the Pharisees fast, but thy disciples fast not?

19 And Jesus said unto them, Can the children of the bridechamber fast, while the bridegroom is with them? as long as they have the bridegroom with them, they cannot fast.

20 But the days will come, when the bridegroom shall be taken away from them, and then shall they fast in those days.

Then, He begins to teach the crowd. Verses 21-22:

21 No man also seweth a piece of new cloth on an old garment: else the new piece that filled it up taketh away from the old, and the rent [rip] is made worse.

22 And no man putteth new wine into

old bottles: else the new wine doth burst the bottles, and the wine is spilled, and the bottles will be marred: but new wine must be put into new bottles.

Jesus was saying that something new was coming to them and it could not be incorporated into the existing religious system.

Always under the critical eyes of the religious leaders, they saw Jesus walking through a cornfield and He was hungry. Verses 23-26:

23 And it came to pass, that he went through the corn fields on the sabbath day; and his disciples began, as they went, to pluck the ears of corn.

24 And the Pharisees said unto him, Behold, why do they on the sabbath day that which is not lawful?

25 And he said unto them, Have ye never read what David did, when he had need, and was an hungred, he, and they that were with him? 26 How he went into the house of God in the days of Abiathar the high priest, and did eat the

shewbread, which is not lawful to eat but for the priests, and gave also to them which were with him?

When God created the world, He did it in six days. On the seventh day, He rested. Genesis 2:1-3:

1 Thus the heavens and the earth were finished, and all the host of them.

2 And on the seventh day God ended his work which he had made; and he rested on the seventh day from all his work which he had made.

3 And God blessed the seventh day, and sanctified it: because that in it he had rested from all his work which God created and made.

Israel was commanded to honor the Sabbath as a day of rest and to keep it holy or separated. Mark 2:27-28:

27 And he said unto them, The sabbath was made for man, and not man for the sabbath: 28 Therefore the Son of man is Lord also of the sabbath.

4

Mark 3

Jesus would often go to the local synagogue to teach. It was the center of religious education and worship for the Jewish community. It would be the most expedient way to reach the Jews. Mark 3:1-4:

1 And he entered again into the synagogue; and there was a man there which had a withered hand. 2 And they watched him, [to see] whether he would heal him on the sabbath day; that they might accuse him.

3 And he saith unto the man which had the withered hand, Stand forth. 4 And he saith unto them, Is it lawful to do good on the sabbath days, or to do evil? to save life, or to kill? But they held their peace [said nothing].

We see a clear division within Israel as Jesus continues to teach them. There are those who have faith and those who do not. This will be the great differentiation. Watch what happens when Jesus heals this man. Verse 5:

> 5 And when he had looked round about on them with anger, being grieved for the hardness of their hearts, he saith unto the man, Stretch forth thine hand. And he stretched it out: and his hand was restored whole as the other.

Notice the response of the religious leaders. Their hearts are filled with anger to the point where they seek to eliminate this threat to their religious system. This was the beginning of His opposition. Verse 6:

> 6 And the Pharisees went forth, and straightway took counsel with the Herodians against him, how they might destroy him.

The crowds had come from far and wide and become quite large. Verses 7-8:

> 7 But Jesus withdrew himself with his disciples to the sea: and a great multitude from Galilee followed him, and

from Judaea, 8 And from Jerusalem, and from Idumaea, and from beyond Jordan; and they about Tyre and Sidon, a great multitude, when they had heard what great things he did, came unto him.

Jesus spoke to His disciples privately. He desired to separate Himself from the crowd. Verses 9-10

9 And he spake to his disciples, that a small ship should wait on him because of the multitude, lest they should throng him.

10 For he had healed many; insomuch that they pressed upon him for to touch him, as many as had plagues.

Here, I want to mention that we are not alone. There is an invisible realm. It is the spiritual realm and it is not visible to the human eye. I think if we could see it, we would be terrified. The Apostle Paul writes in Ephesians 6:12:

12 For we wrestle not against flesh and blood, but against principalities, against powers, against the rulers of the darkness of this world, against spiritual

wickedness in high places.

What we can see is the manifestation of this unseen realm who are very much aware of Who Jesus Christ is. Mark 3:11-12:

> 11 And unclean spirits [demons], when they saw him, fell down before him, and cried, saying, Thou art the Son of God. 12 And he straitly [immediately] charged them that they should not make him known.

In a private conversation, Jesus gives His disciples authority to preach and to heal the sick. He did this so that the people will know that they were sent by Jesus. Verses 13-15:

> 13 And he goeth up into a mountain, and calleth unto him whom he would: and they came unto him.

> 14 And he ordained twelve, that they should be with him, and that he might send them forth to preach, 15 And to have power to heal sicknesses, and to cast out devils [demons]:

In the following, we are given a list of the Twelve

Apostles who were commissioned. Notice that Mark is not included in this list. Verses 16-19:

> 16 **And Simon he surnamed Peter; 17 And James the son of Zebedee, and John the brother of James; and he surnamed them Boanerges, which is, The sons of thunder:**
>
> 18 **And Andrew, and Philip, and Bartholomew, and Matthew, and Thomas, and James the son of Alphaeus, and Thaddaeus, and Simon the Canaanite,**
>
> 19 **And Judas Iscariot, which also betrayed him: and they went into an house.**

While in this house, crowds of people gathered outside hoping to see and hear Jesus. Verses 20-21:

> 20 **And the multitude cometh together again, so that they could not so much as eat bread. 21 And when his friends heard of it, they went out to lay hold on him: for they said, He is beside himself.**

Rarely was Jesus not observed by the religious authorities. In fact, some of them had come from headquarters in Jerusalem. They accused Jesus of using the power of Beelzebub which is a name for Satan, the prince of demons. Verse 22:

> 22 And the scribes which came down from Jerusalem said, He hath Beelzebub, and by the prince of the devils casteth he out devils.

Hearing this preposterous accusation, Jesus responds. The following verses provide an important explanation of a future event. Notice that Jesus is specifically speaking to the religious leaders as representatives of Israel. Verses 23-29:

> 23 And he called them unto him, and said unto them in parables, How can Satan cast out Satan? 24 And if a kingdom be divided against itself, that kingdom cannot stand.

> 25 And if a house be divided against itself, that house cannot stand. 26 And if Satan rise up against himself, and be divided, he cannot stand, but hath an end.

> 27 No man can enter into a strong man's house, and spoil his goods, except he

will first bind the strong man; and then he will spoil his house.

28 Verily I say unto you, All sins shall be forgiven unto the sons of men, and blasphemies wherewith soever they shall blaspheme: 29 <u>But he that shall blaspheme against the Holy Ghost hath never forgiveness, but is in danger of eternal damnation:</u>

What sin would cause this and result in such a dire consequence? Jesus has the holy Spirit of God. They called the Holy Spirit "an unclean spirit" which is the spirit of the Antichrist. Verse 30:

30 Because they [the religion leaders] said, He [Jesus] hath an unclean spirit.

There are some who teach that Mary had no other children and that Jesus had no other half-siblings. While Jesus was teaching, He is informed that His mother and brethren are outside and would like to see Him. Verses 31-32:

31 There came then his brethren and his mother, and, standing without [outside], sent unto him, calling him.

32 And the multitude sat about him, and they said unto him, Behold, thy mother and thy brethren without seek for thee.

Notice His response, but this will need some discussion. Jesus is not denying their biological connection. Let us look at two biblical references that support this. Matthew 13:55-56:

55 Is not this the carpenter's son? is not his mother called Mary? and his brethren, James, and Joses, and Simon, and Judas? 56 And his sisters, are they not all with us? Whence then hath this man all these things?

A similar verse appears in Mark 6:3:

3 Is not this the carpenter, the son of Mary, the brother of James, and Joses, and of Juda, and Simon? and are not his sisters here with us? And they were offended at him.

We must remember that Jesus is a direct descendent of both Abraham and King David. (See Matthew 1:1.) I believe He is not denying His relationship to His biological family. He is stating the importance of the children of Abraham who believe the Gospel of the Kingdom and claims them to be His family. Mark 3:33-35:

> 33 And he answered them, saying, Who is my mother, or my brethren?
>
> 34 And he looked round about on them which sat about him, and said, Behold my mother and my brethren! 35 <u>For whosoever shall do the will of God, the same is my brother, and my sister, and mother.</u>

5

Mark 4

Jesus found it easier to speak to the people outside of the cities. There were beautiful places along the shore of the Sea of Galilee where He could teach. He was able to distance Himself from the crowd by using a ship. Mark 4:1:

> 1 **And he began again to teach by the sea side: and there was gathered unto him a great multitude, so that he entered into a ship, and sat in the sea; and the whole multitude was by the sea on the land.**

Jesus used parables which are stories that contain a lesson easily relatable to those hearing the story. He used common activities and experiences. The stories were intended to teach truths in simple terms to those who heard them. However, many did not understand the lessons. Verse 2:

2 And he taught them many things by parables, and said unto them in his doctrine,

Here is the first parable Mark records in verses 3-9:

3 Hearken; Behold, there went out a sower to sow:

4 And it came to pass, as he sowed, some [seed] fell by the way side, and the fowls of the air came and devoured it up.

5 And some fell on stony ground, where it had not much earth; and immediately it sprang up, because it had no depth of earth: 6 But when the sun was up, it was scorched; and because it had no root, it withered away.

7 And some fell among thorns, and the thorns grew up, and choked it, and it yielded no fruit.

8 And other fell on good ground, and did yield fruit that sprang up and increased; and brought forth, some thirty, and some sixty, and some an hundred.

9 And he said unto them, He that hath ears to hear, let him hear.

Often, the disciples would ask for an explanation. Verses 10-13:

10 And when he was alone, they that were about him with the twelve asked of him the parable.

11 And he said unto them, Unto you it is given to know the mystery of <u>the kingdom of God</u>: but unto them that are without, all these things are done in parables:

12 That seeing they may see, and not perceive; and hearing they may hear, and not understand; lest at any time they should be converted, and their sins should be forgiven them.

13 And he said unto them, Know ye not this parable? and how then will ye know all parables?

He asks them if they do not understand this parable, then how will they understand the other parables. He offers them this explanation. Verses 14-20:

14 The sower soweth the word.

15 And these are they by the way side, where the word is sown; but when they have heard, Satan cometh immediately, and taketh away the word that was sown in their hearts.

16 And these are they likewise which are sown on stony ground; who, when they have heard the word, immediately receive it with gladness; 17 And have no root in themselves, and so endure but for a time: afterward, when affliction or persecution ariseth for the word's sake, immediately they are offended.

18 And these are they which are sown among thorns; such as hear the word, 19 And the cares of this world, and the deceitfulness of riches, and the lusts of other things entering in, choke the word, and it becometh unfruitful.

20 And these are they which are sown on good ground; such as hear the word, and receive it, and bring forth fruit, some thirtyfold, some sixty, and some an hundred.

Jesus uses another parable. This teaches about the light or having knowledge of the truth. What one does with that truth matters. Verses 21-22:

> 21 And he said unto them, Is a candle brought to be put under a bushel, or under a bed? and not to be set on a candlestick?

> 22 For there is nothing hid, which shall not be manifested [made known]; neither was any thing kept secret, but that it should come abroad.

He warns the hearers to pay attention to what they hear to avoid the consequences. Verses 23-25:

> 23 If any man have ears to hear, let him hear.

> 24 And he said unto them, Take heed what ye hear: with what measure ye mete [measure out], it shall be measured [out] to you: and unto you that hear shall more be given.

> 25 For he that hath, to him shall be given: and he that hath not, from him shall be taken even that which he hath.

The previous verses refer to faith or believing God's Word. It is telling them that those who have faith, more will be obtained. To those who do not have faith, they will eventually lose what little faith they have.

This is an important point. Throughout the Old Testament, God was continually teaching Israel to have faith. They would have faith. Then, they would lose and rebel against God. Let us consider the mustard seed in Matthew 17:20:

> 20 **And Jesus said unto them, Because of your unbelief: for verily I say unto you, <u>If ye have faith as a grain of mustard seed, ye shall say unto this mountain, Remove hence to yonder place; and it shall remove; and nothing shall be impossible unto you.</u>**

He is not talking about an exorbitant amount of faith. Consider the size of a mustard seed!

We return to our text. Mark 4:26-29:

> 26 **And he said, So is <u>the kingdom of God</u>, as if a man should cast seed into the ground; 27 And should sleep, and rise night and day, and the seed should**

spring and grow up, he knoweth not how.

28 For the earth bringeth forth fruit of [by] herself; first the blade, then the ear, after that the full corn in the ear.

29 But when the fruit is brought forth, immediately he putteth in the sickle, because the harvest is come.

Consider the word "harvest" as we will see in again relative to the harvest of believers.

Jesus continued to use similar parables to teach them about the kingdom of God. Verses 30-33:

30 And he said, Whereunto shall we liken the kingdom of God? or with what comparison shall we compare it?

31 It is like a grain of mustard seed, which, when it is sown in the earth, is less than [smallest of] all the seeds that be in the earth: 32 But when it is sown, it groweth up, and becometh greater than all herbs, and shooteth out great branches; so that the fowls of the air may lodge under the shadow of it.

33 And with many such [similar] parables spake he the word unto them, as they were able to hear it.

The mass of people found understanding these parables difficult. Jesus would take His disciples aside and explain them. Verse 34:

34 But without a parable spake he not unto them: and when they were alone, he expounded all things to his disciples.

Still on the shore of the Sea of Galilee, they decided to go from one shore to another by ship. They were accompanied by other ships that traveled along with them. Verses 35-36:

35 And the same day, when the even [evening] was come, he saith unto them, Let us pass over unto the other side.

36 And when they had sent away the multitude, they took him even as he was in the ship. And there were also with him other little ships.

Can you imagine having the peace of God and being able to sleep through a storm? Such was the case with Jesus Who slept in the ship while a storm

42

raged. Filled with water, the ship was floundering in the waves. Verses 37-38:

> 37 And there arose a great storm of wind, and the waves beat into the ship, so that it was now full.

> 38 And he was in the hinder [rear] part of the ship, asleep on a pillow: and they awake him, and say unto him, Master, carest thou not that we perish?

It appears that they had not fully realized, up to this point, Who Jesus is. Notice Jesus' response. Verses 39-41:

> 39 And he arose, and rebuked the wind, and said unto the sea, Peace, be still. And the wind ceased, and there was a great calm.

> 40 And he said unto them, <u>Why are ye so fearful? how is it that ye have no faith?</u>

> 41 And they feared exceedingly, and said one to another, <u>What manner of man is this, that even the wind and the sea obey him?</u>

6

Mark 5

One benefit of studying the synoptic gospels is that the same story is often recorded from different perspectives. Mosaic Law requires testimony from two or more witnesses. Such is the case with the life and teachings of Jesus Christ. One event involved the casting out of demons. There was a man who had many demons who called themselves "Legion." This was also recorded in Matthew 28:8-34 and Luke 8:26-37. You can compare them with Mark's record. Mark 5:1-1-4:

> 1 **And they came over unto the other side of the sea, into the country of the Gadarenes.**
>
> 2 **And when he was come out of the ship, immediately there met him out of**

the tombs a man with an unclean spirit [demon],

> 3 Who had his dwelling among the tombs; and no man could bind him, no, not with chains: 4 Because that he had been often bound with fetters and chains, and the chains had been plucked asunder by him, and the fetters broken in pieces: neither could any man tame him.

This individual was well known by the local people who chose to avoid contact with this lunatic. Verse 5:

> 5 And always, night and day, he was in the mountains, and in the tombs, crying, and cutting himself with stones.

We see that the demon knew Who Jesus was. Verses 6-7:

> 6 But when he saw Jesus afar off, he ran and worshipped him, 7 And cried with a loud voice, and said, What have I to do with thee, <u>Jesus, thou Son of the most high God</u>? I adjure [plead] thee by God, that thou torment me not.

Jesus exercises His divine authority and the demon obeys. Verses 8-13:

> 8 **For he said unto him, Come out of the man, thou unclean spirit. 9 And he asked him, What is thy name? And he answered, saying, My name is Legion: for we are many. 10 And he besought [begged] him much that he [Jesus] would not send them [many demons] away out of the country.**

> 11 **Now there was there nigh [nearby] unto the mountains a great herd of swine feeding. 12 And all the devils besought [begged] him, saying, Send us into the swine, that we may enter into them.**

> 13 **And forthwith [immediately] Jesus gave them leave. And the unclean spirits went out, and entered into the swine: and the herd ran violently down a steep place into the sea, (they were about two thousand;) and were choked in the sea.**

This did not happen secretly, but out in the open. It was observed by bystanders namely those who tended the swine. News spread throughout the countryside so that many came out to see what had happened. There was much evidence as to what occurred. The dead carcasses of the swine were still floating in the sea. The lunatic, known by all, was in his right mind. And, there was Jesus in the midst of this. Verses 14-15:

> 14 And they that fed the swine fled, and told it in the city, and in the country. And they went out to see what it was that was done.

> 15 And they come to Jesus, and see him that was possessed with the devil, and had the legion, sitting, and clothed, and in his right mind: and they were afraid.

Notice the reaction of the local people. Evidence of the miracle was plentiful, but they chose fear over faith and asked Jesus to leave. Verses 16-17:

> 16 And they that saw it told them how it befell to him that was possessed with the devil, and also concerning the swine. 17 And they began to pray him to depart out of their coasts.

As Jesus was departing their region by ship, the man who was healed came to Jesus asking to go with Him. Yet, it was better for the man to remain as a testimony to his neighbors of what the grace of God can do. Verses 18-20:

> 18 And when he was come into the ship, he that had been possessed with the devil prayed [asked] him that he might be with him. 19 Howbeit Jesus suffered [allowed] him not, but saith unto him, Go home to thy friends, and tell them how great things the Lord hath done for thee, and hath had compassion on thee.

> 20 And he [man] departed, and began to publish [make known] in Decapolis how great things Jesus had done for him: and all men did marvel.

Leaving the region of the Gadarenes, Jesus crossed from one side of the Sea of Galilee to the other. When He arrived He was greeted by one of the religious rulers of Israel. However, the ruler came not to judge Him but desiring His help. Verses 21-24:

> 21 And when Jesus was passed over again by ship unto the other side, much people gathered unto him: and he was nigh unto the sea. 22 And, behold, there-recometh one of the rulers of the syna-

gogue, Jairus by name; and when he saw him, he fell at his feet,

23 And besought [begged] him greatly, saying, My little daughter lieth at the point of death: I pray thee, come and lay thy hands on her, that she may be healed; and she shall live.

24 And Jesus went with him; and much people followed him, and thronged him.

On their way to heal Jairus' daughter, they are interrupted by another person who desperately needs Jesus' healing. Verses 25-28:

25 And a certain woman, which had an issue of blood twelve years, 26 And had suffered many things of many physicians, and had spent all that she had, and was nothing bettered, but rather grew worse,

27 When she had heard of Jesus, came in the press [crowd] behind, and touched his garment. 28 For she said, If I may touch but his clothes, I shall be whole.

Notice that her action was based upon her faith in Who Jesus is and in His ability to heal her. Verses 29-34:

> 29 And straightway the fountain of her blood was dried up; and she felt in her body that she was healed of that plague.
>
> 30 And Jesus, immediately knowing in himself that virtue had gone out of him, turned him about in the press [crowd], and said, Who touched my clothes?
>
> 31 And his disciples said unto him, Thou seest the multitude thronging thee, and sayest thou, Who touched me? 32 And he looked round about to see her that had done this thing.
>
> 33 But the woman fearing and trembling, knowing what was done in her, came and fell down before him, and told him all the truth.
>
> 34 And he said unto her, Daughter, thy faith hath made thee whole; go in peace, and be whole of thy plague.

All this happened as they walked to Jairus'

house. Verses 35-36:

> 35 While he yet spake, there came from the ruler of the synagogue's house certain which said, Thy daughter is dead: why troublest thou the Master any further?

> 36 As soon as Jesus heard the word that was spoken, he saith unto the ruler of the synagogue, Be not afraid, only believe.

Remember this. Faith is the key! The ruler must have faith in the same manner as the woman who touched His garments and was healed. Verses 37-43:

> 37 And he [Jesus] suffered {allowed] no man to follow him, save [except] Peter, and James, and John the brother of James.

> 38 And he cometh to the house of the ruler of the synagogue, and seeth the tumult, and them that wept and wailed greatly.

> 39 And when he was come in, he saith unto them, Why make ye this ado, and

weep? the damsel is not dead, but sleepeth.

40 <u>And they laughed him to scorn.</u> But when he had put them all out, he taketh the father and the mother of the damsel, and them that were with him, and entereth in where the damsel was lying.

41 And he took the damsel by the hand, and said unto her, Talitha cumi; which is, being interpreted, Damsel, I say unto thee, arise.

42 And straightway the damsel arose, and walked; for she was of the age of twelve years. And they were astonished with a great astonishment.

43 And he charged them straitly that no man should know it; and commanded that something should be given her to eat.

Jairus, a ruler of Israel, witnessed not once but twice the healing miracles of Jesus Christ — the Messiah and the Son of God!

7

Mark 6

Leaving behind Jairus' family rejoicing over the healing of his daughter, Jesus went to His home synagogue in Nazareth. Again, we will see the importance of faith. Mark 6:1-3:

1 **And he went out from thence, and came into his own country; and his disciples follow him.**

2 **And when the sabbath day was come, he began to teach in the synagogue: and many hearing him were astonished, saying, From whence hath this man these things? and what wisdom is this which is given unto him, that even such mighty works are wrought by his hands?**

3 Is not this the carpenter, the son of Mary, the brother of James, and Joses, and of Juda, and Simon? and are not his sisters here with us? And they were offended at him.

People are so easily offended. Such was the case with those who knew Jesus as a boy. Yet, Jesus was not surprised. Verse 4:

4 But Jesus said unto them, A prophet is not without honour, but in his own country, and among his own kin, and in his own house.

Notice the result of their lack of faith. Verses 5-6:

5 And he could there do no mighty work, save that he laid his hands upon a few sick folk, and healed them.

6 And he marvelled because of their unbelief. And he went round about the villages, teaching.

The disciples had been with Jesus for some time and they were ready to be sent out. He chose to send them in pairs so that they could encourage each other while preaching the Gospel of the Kingdom.

Verses 7-10:

> 7 And he called unto him the twelve, and began to send them forth by two and two; and gave them power over unclean spirits;

> 8 And commanded them that they should take nothing for their journey, save a staff only; no scrip, no bread, no money in their purse: 9 But be shod with sandals; and not put on two coats.

> 10 And he said unto them, In what place soever ye enter into an house, there abide till ye depart from that place.

They are not to be disheartened by those who choose to ignore or reject the gospel. The gospel is light. Some will choose the darkness. Verse 11:

> 11 And whosoever shall not receive you, nor hear you, when ye depart thence, shake off the dust under your feet for a testimony against them. Verily I say unto you, It shall be more tolerable for Sodom and Gomorrha in the day of judgment, than for that city.

The Twelve did as the Lord instructed. They went out proclaiming the good news of the coming Kingdom. Verses 12-13:

> 12 **And they went out, and preached that men should repent.** 13 **And they cast out many devils, and anointed with oil many that were sick, and healed them.**

King Herod had killed John the Baptist as we see in the text below. Herod believed that John had risen from the dead. Verses 14-28:

> 14 **And king Herod heard of him; (for his name was spread abroad:) and he said, That John the Baptist was risen from the dead, and therefore mighty works do shew forth themselves in him.**
>
> 15 **Others said, That it is Elias. And others said, That it is a prophet, or as one of the prophets.**
>
> 16 **But when Herod heard thereof, he said, It is John, whom I beheaded: he is risen from the dead.** 17 **For Herod himself had sent forth and laid hold upon John, and bound him in prison for Herodias' sake, his brother Philip's wife:**

for he had married her. 18 For John had said unto Herod, It is not lawful for thee to have thy brother's wife.

19 Therefore Herodias had a quarrel against him [John the Baptist], and would have killed him; but she could not: 20 For Herod feared John, knowing that he was a just man and an holy, and observed him; and when he heard him, he did many things, and heard him gladly.

21 And when a convenient day was come, that Herod on his birthday made a supper to his lords, high captains, and chief estates of Galilee;

22 And when the daughter of the said Herodias came in, and danced, and pleased Herod and them that sat with him, the king said unto the damsel, Ask of me whatsoever thou wilt, and I will give it thee. 23 And he sware unto her, Whatsoever thou shalt ask of me, I will give it thee, unto the half of my kingdom.

24 And she went forth, and said unto her

mother, What shall I ask? And she said, The head of John the Baptist.

25 And she came in straightway with haste unto the king, and asked, saying, I will that thou give me by and by in a charger [on a platter] the head of John the Baptist.

26 And the king was exceeding sorry; yet for his oath's sake, and for their sakes which sat with him, he would not reject her. 27 And immediately the king sent an executioner, and commanded his head to be brought: and he went and beheaded him in the prison,

28 And brought his head in a charger, and gave it to the damsel: and the damsel gave it to her mother.

News of this came to the disciples of John the Baptist and they mourned the loss of their friend and teacher. Verses 29-31:

29 And when his disciples heard of it, they came and took up his corpse, and laid it in a tomb. 30 And the apostles gathered themselves together unto

Jesus, and told him all things, both what they had done, and what they had taught.

31 And he said unto them, Come ye yourselves apart into a desert [deserted] place, and rest a while: for there were many coming and going, and they had no leisure so much as to eat.

The Twelve were weary from the work and the crowds so that Jesus took them to an isolated place where they could eat and rest.

Using a ship, they went to a place where they could be alone. However, it was not long before the crowds found them. Verses 32-34:

32 And they departed into a desert [deserted] place by ship privately. 33 And the people saw them departing, and many knew him, and ran afoot thither out of all cities, and outwent them, and came together unto him.

34 And Jesus, when he came out, saw much people, and was moved with compassion toward them, because <u>they were as sheep not having a shepherd</u>:

and he began to teach them many things.

Jesus spent the majority of the day teaching the crowd until late afternoon. Evening would arrive soon. It was a beautiful site overlooking the Sea of Galilee. The disciples suggested that Jesus send the people away because there was no food in this remote place. Verses 35-38:

35 And when the day was now far spent, his disciples came unto him, and said, This is a desert place, and now the time is far passed: 36 Send them away, that they may go into the country round about, and into the villages, and buy themselves bread: for they have nothing to eat.

37 He answered and said unto them, Give ye them to eat. And they say unto him, Shall we go and buy two hundred pennyworth of bread, and give them to eat?

38 He saith unto them, How many loaves have ye? go and see. And when they knew, they say, Five, and two fishes.

Looking out over the crowd, He saw a vast sea of men women and children. Jesus instructed them to sit down on the grass forming groups. Of the men alone, there were five thousand. Then, Jesus instructed the Twelve to distribute the meager amount of food that they had. Verses 39-44:

> 39 And he commanded them to make all sit down by companies upon the green grass. 40 And they sat down in ranks, by hundreds, and by fifties.
>
> 41 And when he had taken the five loaves and the two fishes, he looked up to heaven, and blessed, and brake the loaves, and gave them to his disciples to set before them; and the two fishes divided he among them all.
>
> 42 And they did all eat, and were filled. 43 And they took up twelve baskets full of the fragments, and of the fishes. 44 And they that did eat of the loaves were about five thousand men.

After feeding the people, Jesus remained to dismiss them. He sent the disciples by ship to Bethsaida where He would meet them as He desired to be alone. Verses 45-46:

45 And straightway he constrained his disciples to get into the ship, and to go to the other side before unto Bethsaida, while he sent away the people.

46 And when he had sent them away, he departed into a mountain to pray.

While Jesus remained to pray, the disciples were on the ship heading to their destination where they would meet Jesus. Verse 47:

47 And when even [evening] was come, the ship was in the midst of the sea, and he alone on the land.

The fourth watch is between 3 AM and 6 AM. The disciples were struggling on the ship as they were heading into the wind. They looked and saw Jesus walking on the water on His way to Bethsaida. Verses 48-50:

48 And he saw them toiling in rowing; for the wind was contrary unto them: and about the fourth watch of the night he cometh unto them, walking upon the sea, and would have passed by them.

49 But when they saw him walking upon

the sea, they supposed it had been a spirit, and cried out:

50 For they all saw him, and were troubled. And immediately he talked with them, and saith unto them, Be of good cheer: it is I; be not afraid.

When Jesus joined them in the ship, the strong winds ceased. Verse 51:

51 And he went up unto them into the ship; and the wind ceased: and they were sore amazed in themselves beyond measure, and wondered.

The text tells us that they did not think much about the miracle of the loaves and fish. It says that their hearts were hardened. Even after all this time, they did not understand because of their lack of faith. Verse 52:

52 For they considered not the miracle of the loaves: for their heart was hardened.

Gennesaret is located on the northwestern shore of the Sea of Galilee not far from Capernaum. When they arrived, Jesus was immediately recognized. Verses 53-54:

53 And when they had passed over, they came into the land of Gennesaret, and drew to the shore. 54 And when they were come out of the ship, straightway they knew him,

News spread quickly throughout the region. As He traveled, they brought the sick to Him to be healed. Verses 55-56:

55 And ran through that whole region round about, and began to carry about in beds those that were sick, where they heard he was.

56 And whithersoever he entered, into villages, or cities, or country, they laid the sick in the streets, and besought him that they might touch if it were but the border of his garment: and as many as touched him were made whole.

8

Mark 7

A group of religious leaders came from Jerusalem and observed that Jesus' disciples were not keeping the traditions created by the elders. These are the rulers who have added the "traditions of men" to the Laws of God. The Apostle Paul would later warn about this same thing saying, "Beware lest any man spoil you through philosophy and vain deceit, after the tradition of men . . ." (Col. 2:8). Mark 7:1-4:

> 1 Then came together unto him the Pharisees, and certain of the scribes, which came from Jerusalem. 2 And when they saw some of his disciples eat bread with defiled, that is to say, with unwashen, hands, they found fault.

> 3 For the Pharisees, and all the Jews, except they wash their hands oft, eat not,

holding <u>the tradition of the elders</u>.

4 And when they come from the market, except they wash, they eat not. And many other things there be, which they have received to hold, as the washing of cups, and pots, brasen [brass] vessels, and of tables.

The religious leaders had taken the requirements of the Law but added their own. They ask Jesus why His disciples do not observe or honor these traditions. Verses 5-9:

5 Then the Pharisees and scribes asked him, Why walk not thy disciples according to <u>the tradition of the elders</u>, but eat bread with unwashen hands?

6 He answered and said unto them, Well hath Esaias prophesied of you hypocrites, as it is written, This people honoureth me with their lips, but their heart is far from me.

7 Howbeit in vain do they worship me, <u>teaching for doctrines the commandments of men</u>.

8 For laying aside [Ignoring] the commandment of God, ye hold <u>the tradition of men</u>, as the washing of pots and cups: and many other such like things ye do.

9 And he said unto them, Full well <u>ye reject the commandment of God, that ye may keep your own tradition.</u>

He accuses them of ignoring God's commandments and instead keeping their own traditions. He cites examples. Verse 10:

10 For Moses said, Honour thy father and thy mother; and, Whoso curseth father or mother, let him die the death:

The word "Corban" means "a gift or offering to God usually one given to fulfill a vow made." Verses 11-12:

11 But ye say, If a man shall say to his father or mother, It is Corban, that is to say, a gift, by whatsoever thou mightest be profited by me; he shall be free. 12 And ye suffer [allow] him no more to do ought [anything] for his father or his mother;

They have overridden God's Law and made their own law superior to His. Verse 13.

> 13 Making the word of God of none effect [void] through your tradition, which ye have delivered: and many such like things do ye.

Jesus beckons the crowd over and begins to teach them. Verses 14-16:

> 14 And when he had called all the people unto him, he said unto them, Hearken unto me every one of you, and understand:

> 15 There is nothing from without [outside] a man, that entering into him can defile him: but the things which come out of him, those are they that defile the man. 16 If any man have ears to hear, let him hear.

Jesus and His disciples entered into a private home and, when alone inside, they asked Him about this parable. Verses 17-19:

17 And when he was entered into the house [away] from the people, his disciples asked him concerning the parable.

18 And he saith unto them, Are ye so without understanding also? Do ye not perceive, that whatsoever thing from without [outside] entereth into the man, it cannot defile him; 19 Because it entereth not into his heart, but into the belly, and goeth out into the draught [waste], purging all meats [meals]?

It is not what goes into a man that defiles him, but what comes out of the man. Verses 20-23:

20 And he said, That which cometh out of the man, that defileth the man. 21 For from within, out of the heart of men, proceed evil thoughts, adulteries, fornications, murders, 22 Thefts, covetousness, wickedness, deceit, lasciviousness, an evil eye, blasphemy, pride, foolishness:

23 All these evil things come from within, and defile the man.

Jesus and His disciples leave for Tyre and Sidon. Both are port cities on the Mediterranean Sea located in present-day Lebanon. Upon arriving there, He was immediately found by the crowd. Verse 24:

> 24 And from thence he arose, and went into the borders of Tyre and Sidon, and entered into an house, and would have no man know it: but he could not be hid.

The following verses must be seen in their proper context. Jesus came to confirm the promises made to the fathers. (See Romans 15:8.) These promises were made to Abraham and King David both of whom Jesus is their Son. When Jesus sent out the Twelve, He specifically told them not to go the Gentiles, but to the Jews. Matthew 10:5-7:

> 5 These twelve Jesus sent forth, and commanded them, saying, <u>Go not into the way of the Gentiles</u>, and into any city of the Samaritans enter ye not: 6 <u>But go rather to the lost sheep of the house of Israel.</u> 7 <u>And as ye go, preach, saying, The kingdom of heaven is at hand.</u>

By understanding the exclusive nature of Jesus' ministry to the children of Abraham, the following will make sense. Mark 7:25-27:

> 25 **For a certain woman, whose young daughter had an unclean spirit, heard of him, and came and fell at his feet:**
>
> 26 **The woman was a Greek, a Syrophenician by nation; and she besought him that he would cast forth the devil out of her daughter.**
>
> 27 **But Jesus said unto her, Let the children first be filled: for it is not meet [appropriate] to take the children's bread, and to cast it unto the dogs.**

Speaking to this woman, Jesus referred to Gentiles as dogs. He continues with Verses 28-30:

> 28 **And she answered and said unto him, Yes, Lord: yet the dogs under the table eat of the children's crumbs.**
>
> 29 **And he said unto her, For this saying go thy way; the devil is gone out of thy daughter.** 30 **And when she was come to her house, she found the devil [demon] gone out, and her daughter laid upon the bed.**

Jesus left for the region called Decapolis located to the southeast of the Sea of Galilee. Verses 31-37:

> 31 And again, departing from the coasts of Tyre and Sidon, he came unto the sea of Galilee, through the midst of the coasts [shores] of Decapolis.

> 32 And they bring unto him one that was deaf, and had an impediment in his speech; and they beseech him to put his hand upon him. 33 And he took him aside from the multitude, and put his fingers into his ears, and he spit, and touched his tongue;

> 34 And looking up to heaven, he sighed, and saith unto him, Ephphatha, that is, Be opened. 35 And straightway his ears were opened, and the string of his tongue was loosed, and he spake plain.

> 36 And he charged them that they should tell no man: but the more he charged them, so much the more a great deal they published it;

> 37 And were beyond measure aston-

ished, saying, He hath done all things well: he maketh both the deaf to hear, and the dumb to speak.

9

Mark 8

Those who received healing were instructed by Jesus not to tell anyone, but they could not contain themselves. His popularity grew. The religious leaders played an important and dominant role in the Jewish culture. Jesus was now in the spotlight and they did not like that. Mark 8:1-4:

1 In those days the multitude being very great, and having nothing to eat, Jesus called his disciples unto him, and saith unto them, 2 I have compassion on the multitude, because they have now been with me three days, and have nothing to eat:

3 And if I send them away fasting [not having eaten] to their own houses, they will faint by the way: for divers [differ-

ent ones] of them came from far.

4 And his disciples answered him, From whence can a man satisfy these men with bread here in the wilderness?

In Matthew, Jesus told His disciples, "With men this is impossible; but with God all things are possible" (Matt. 19:26). Here again, Jesus will do another miracle by feeding the multitude. Perhaps, this time, the disciples' hearts will not be hardened. Verses 5-9:

5 And he asked them, How many loaves have ye? And they said, Seven.

6 And he commanded the people to sit down on the ground: and he took the seven loaves, and gave thanks, and brake, and gave to his disciples to set before them; and they did set them before the people.

7 And they had a few small fishes: and he blessed, and commanded to set them also before them. 8 So they did eat, and were filled: and they took up of the broken meat that was left seven baskets.

9 And they that had eaten were about four thousand: and he sent them away.

Following this miracle, Jesus again leaves by the ship to Dalmanutha also on the shore of the Sea of Galilee. There he is greeted by Pharisees who came to question Him. Verses 10-13:

10 And straightway [immediately] he entered into a ship with his disciples, and came into the parts of Dalmanutha.

11 And the Pharisees came forth, and began to question with him, seeking of him a sign from heaven, tempting him.

12 And he sighed deeply in his spirit, and saith, Why doth this generation seek after a sign? verily I say unto you, There shall no sign be given unto this generation.

13 And he left them, and entering into the ship again departed to the other side.

It appears that the following conversation took place on the ship. Still working with His disciples, it appears that they still have not learned from all that has occurred. Verses 14-21:

14 Now the disciples had forgotten to take bread, neither had they in the ship with them more than one loaf.

15 And he charged them, saying, Take heed, beware of the leaven of the Pharisees, and of the leaven of Herod. 16 And they reasoned among themselves, saying, It is because we have no bread.

17 And when Jesus knew it, he saith unto them, Why reason ye, because ye have no bread? perceive ye not yet, neither understand? have ye your heart yet hardened? 18 Having eyes, see ye not? and having ears, hear ye not? and do ye not remember?

19 When I brake the five loaves among five thousand, how many baskets full of fragments took ye up? They say unto him, Twelve. 20 And when the seven among four thousand, how many baskets full of fragments took ye up? And they said, Seven.

21 And he said unto them, How is it that ye do not understand?

The ship arrived in Bethsaida on the northeastern shore of the Sea of Galilee. Verses 22-26:

22 And he cometh to Bethsaida; and they bring a blind man unto him, and besought him to touch him. **23** And he took the blind man by the hand, and led him out of the town; and when he had spit on his eyes, and put his hands upon him, he asked him if he saw ought [anything].

24 And he looked up, and said, I see men as trees, walking. **25** After that he put his hands again upon his eyes, and made him look up: and he was restored, and saw every man clearly. **26** And he sent him away to his house, saying, Neither go into the town, nor tell it to any in the town.

Caesarea Philippi is located on the northern part of the Sea of Galilee in the foothills of Mount Hermon. As they travel, Jesus asks His disciples who do people say that He is. Verses 27-30:

27 And Jesus went out, and his disciples, into the towns of Caesarea Philippi: and by [along] the way he asked his disciples, saying unto them, Whom do men say that I am?

28 And they answered, John the Baptist: but some say, Elias; and others, One of the prophets.

29 And he saith unto them, But whom say ye that I am? And Peter answereth and saith unto him, <u>Thou art the Christ.</u>

30 And he charged them that they should tell no man of him.

It appears from this that the general populace had no idea Who Jesus Christ is. Yet, Peter gives a bold proclamation. He instructs them to keep His identity a secret for now. The Gospel of Matthew provides us with additional details. Matthew 16:16-17:

16 And Simon Peter answered and said, <u>Thou art the Christ, the Son of the living God.</u>

17 And Jesus answered and said unto

him, Blessed art thou, Simon Barjona: for <u>flesh and blood hath not revealed it unto thee, but my Father which is in heaven.</u>

The Holy Spirit inspires the writing of the Word. Also, the Holy Spirit illuminates the Word for our understanding.

Jesus teaches His disciples about what must happen to Him as the Son of Man. Mark 8:31-32:

> 31 And he began to teach them, that the Son of man must suffer many things, and be rejected of the elders, and of the chief priests, and scribes, and be killed, and after three days rise again.
>
> 32 And he spake that saying openly. And Peter took him, and began to rebuke him.

Many have speculated as to why Peter rebuked Jesus, perhaps he just did not want his Friend to be killed. Jesus rejected Peter's statement. Verse 33:

> 33 But when he had turned about and looked on his disciples, he rebuked Peter, saying, Get thee behind me, Satan:

for thou savourest [understand] not the things that be of God, but the things that be of men.

Jesus beckons to the crowds and begins to teach them again. Verses 34-38:

34 And when he had called the people unto him with his disciples also, he said unto them, Whosoever will come after me, let him deny himself, and take up his cross, and follow me.

35 For whosoever will save his life shall lose it; but whosoever shall lose his life for my sake and the gospel's, the same shall save it. 36 For what shall it profit a man, if he shall gain the whole world, and lose his own soul? 37 Or what shall a man give in exchange for his soul?

38 Whosoever therefore shall be ashamed of me and of my words in this adulterous and sinful generation; of him also shall the Son of man be ashamed, when he cometh in the glory of his Father with the holy angels.

10

Mark 9

As mentioned before, the first three gospels are synoptic gospels and share details of many of the same events. The following is Mark's record of the Transfiguration of the Christ. Similar details are provided by Matthew 17:1-9 and Luke 9:28-36. We begin with Mark 9:1:

> 1 **And he [Jesus] said unto them, Verily I say unto you, That there be some of them that stand here, which shall not taste of death, till they have seen <u>the kingdom of God</u> come with power.**

He was speaking of the Transfiguration. A king is anointed which symbolizes that he is set apart by God. After that, there is the crowning. In the following, the Messiah takes on this anointing before two witnesses: Moses and Elijah. Verse 2:

2 And after six days Jesus taketh with him Peter, and James, and John, and leadeth them up into an high mountain apart by themselves: and he was transfigured before them.

These three disciples saw "the kingdom of God come with power" (v. 1). Verses 3-9:

3 And his raiment became shining, exceeding white as snow; so as no fuller on earth can white them. 4 And there appeared unto them Elias with Moses: and they were talking with Jesus.

5 And Peter answered and said to Jesus, Master, it is good for us to be here: and let us make three tabernacles; one for thee, and one for Moses, and one for Elias. 6 For he wist [knew] not what to say; for they were sore afraid.

7 And there was a cloud that overshadowed them: and a voice came out of the cloud, saying, This is my beloved Son: hear him.

8 And suddenly, when they had looked round about, they saw no man anymore,

**save [except] Jesus only with them-
selves.**

**9 And as they came down from the
mountain, he charged them that they
should tell no man what things they
had seen, till the Son of man were risen
from the dead.**

It will be apparent that these three did not understand, but they would later. In the meantime, they
are told to keep this matter in confidence. Verse 10:

**10 And they kept that saying with them-
selves, questioning one with another
what the rising from the dead should
mean.**

Many Jews believed that before the Messiah
would come, that Elijah must precede Him. So, they
ask Jesus if this is the case. Verses 11-13:

**11 And they asked him, saying, Why say
the scribes that Elias must first come?**

**12 And he answered and told them, Elias
verily cometh first, and restoreth all
things; and how it is written of the Son
of man, that he must suffer many**

things, and be set at nought [nothing].

13 But I say unto you, That Elias is indeed come, and they have done unto him whatsoever they listed, as it is written of him.

In Matthew, Jesus spoke about John the Baptist. Let us compare the texts. Matthew 11:10-15:

10 For this is he, of whom it is written, Behold, I send my messenger before thy face, which shall prepare thy way before thee.

11 Verily I say unto you, Among them that are born of women there hath not risen a greater than John the Baptist: notwithstanding he that is least in the kingdom of heaven is greater than he.

12 And from the days of John the Baptist until now the kingdom of heaven suffereth violence, and the violent take it by force.

13 For all the prophets and the law prophesied until John. 14 And if ye will receive it, this is Elias, which was for to

<u>come</u>. 15 He that hath ears to hear, let him hear.

Upon returning, He found that another crowd had gathered. Mark 9:14-27:

> 14 And when he came to his [other] disciples, he saw a great multitude about them, and the scribes questioning with them. 15 And straightway [immediately] all the people, when they beheld him, were greatly amazed, and running to him saluted [greeted] him. 16 And he asked the scribes, What question ye with them?

> 17 And one of the multitude answered and said, Master, I have brought unto thee my son, which hath a dumb spirit; 18 And wheresoever he taketh him, he teareth him: and he foameth, and gnasheth with his teeth, and pineth away: and I spake to thy disciples that they should cast him out; and they could not.

> 19 He answereth him, and saith, O faithless generation, how long shall I be with you? how long shall I suffer you?

bring him unto me. 20 And they brought him unto him: and when he saw him, straightway [immediately] the spirit tare [tore] him; and he fell on the ground, and wallowed foaming.

21 And he asked his father, How long is it ago since this came unto him? And he said, Of a child. 22 And ofttimes it hath cast him into the fire, and into the waters, to destroy him: but if thou canst [can] do any thing, have compassion on us, and help us.

23 Jesus said unto him, If thou canst [can] believe, all things are possible to him that believeth. 24 And straightway the father of the child cried out, and said with tears, Lord, I believe; help thou mine unbelief.

25 When Jesus saw that the people came running together, he rebuked the foul spirit, saying unto him, Thou dumb and deaf spirit, I charge thee, come out of him, and enter no more into him.

26 And the spirit cried, and rent him sore, and came out of him: and he was

as one dead; insomuch that many said, He is dead. 27 But Jesus took him by the hand, and lifted him up; and he arose.

After the conclusion of this healing, the disciples took Jesus aside and asked Him privately why they could not heal this young man. Verses 28-29:

28 And when he was come into the house, his disciples asked him privately, Why could not we cast him out? 29 And he said unto them, This kind can come forth by nothing, but by prayer and fasting.

Jesus and the disciples left and traveled again. Jesus is fully God and fully man. He was not only weary from all that had just happened, but also from the weight of what would soon happen. He desired to be alone with His disciples. Verses 30-31:

30 And they departed thence, and passed through Galilee; and he would not that any man should know it.

31 For he taught his disciples, and said unto them, <u>The Son of man is delivered into the hands of men, and they shall kill him; and after that he is killed, he</u>

<u>**shall rise the third day.**</u>

Still, they did not understand. Verse 32:

> 32 **But they understood not that saying, and were afraid to ask him.**

As they walked to Capernaum on the shore of the Sea of Galilee, there was a heated discussion among the disciples. Verses 33-35:

> 33 **And he came to Capernaum: and being in the house he asked them, What was it that ye disputed among yourselves by [along] the way?**

> 34 **But they held their peace: for by the way they had disputed among themselves, who should be the greatest.**

> 35 **And he sat down, and called the twelve, and saith unto them, If any man desire to be first, the same shall be last of all, and servant of all.**

As they walked, Jesus sat down and put a nearby child upon His knee. Verses 36-37:

> 36 **And he took a child, and set him in**

the midst of them: and when he had taken him in his arms, he said unto them, 37 Whosoever shall receive one of such children in my name, receiveth me: and whosoever shall receive me, receiveth not me, but him that sent me.

As they walked together, John asked Jesus a question. Verses 38-40:

38 And John answered him, saying, Master, we saw one casting out devils in thy name, and he followeth not us: and we forbad him, because he followeth not us.

39 But Jesus said, Forbid him not: for there is no man which shall do a miracle in my name, that can lightly speak evil of me. 40 For he that is not against us is on our part.

Jesus continues teaching them again referring to the child. Verses 41-42:

41 For whosoever shall give you a cup of water to drink in my name, because ye belong to Christ, verily I say unto you, he shall not lose his reward.

42 And whosoever shall offend one of these little ones that believe in me, it is better for him that a millstone were hanged about his neck, and he were cast into the sea.

I picture the disciples with their eyes upon both Jesus and the child. They listen as He continues. Verses 43-50:

43 And if thy hand offend thee, cut it off: it is better for thee to enter into life maimed, than having two hands to go into hell, into the fire that never shall be quenched: 44 Where their worm dieth not, and the fire is not quenched.

45 And if thy foot offend thee, cut it off: it is better for thee to enter halt into life, than having two feet to be cast into hell, into the fire that never shall be quenched: 46 Where their worm dieth not, and the fire is not quenched.

47 And if thine eye offend thee, pluck it out: it is better for thee to enter into the kingdom of God with one eye, than having two eyes to be cast into hell fire: 48 Where their worm dieth not, and the

fire is not quenched.

49 For every one shall be salted with fire, and every sacrifice shall be salted with salt.

50 Salt is good: but if the salt have lost his saltness, wherewith will ye season it? Have salt in yourselves, and have peace one with another.

11

Mark 10

The words "the coasts of Judaea" mean the central portion of Israel along the Mediterranean coast from Ashdod north to Gaza. It would be about forty miles west of Jerusalem — an estimated two-day journey. Mark 10:1:

> 1 And he arose from thence [that place], and cometh into the coasts of Judaea by the farther side of Jordan: and the people resort [returned] unto him again; and, as he was wont [custom], he taught them again.

There arrived some Pharisees, teachers of the Law, who came to test Jesus according to their customs. Verses 2-9:

> 2 And the Pharisees came to him, and

asked him, Is it lawful for a man to put away his wife? tempting [testing] him.

3 And he answered and said unto them, What did Moses command you? 4 And they said, Moses suffered [allowed] to write a bill of divorcement, and to put her away.

5 And Jesus answered and said unto them, For the hardness of your heart he wrote you this precept. 6 But from [since] the beginning of the creation God made them male and female.

7 For this cause shall a man leave his father and mother, and cleave to his wife; 8 And they twain [two] shall be one flesh: so then they are no more twain [two], but one flesh.

9 What therefore God hath joined together, let not man put asunder.

His disciples asked Jesus to explain this when they were alone with Him. Verses 10-12:

10 And in the house his disciples asked him again of the same matter.

11 And he saith unto them, Whosoever shall put away his wife, and marry another, committeth adultery against her.

12 And if a woman shall put away her husband, and be married to another, she committeth adultery.

Jesus loved little children and likened them to the kingdom of God. Verses 13-16:

13 And they brought young children to him, that he should touch them: and his disciples rebuked those that brought them.

14 But when Jesus saw it, he was much displeased, and said unto them, Suffer [Allow] the little children to come unto me, and forbid them not: for of such is the kingdom of God.

15 Verily I say unto you, Whosoever shall not receive the kingdom of God as a little child, he shall not enter therein.

16 And he took them up in his arms, put his hands upon them, and blessed them.

He left with His disciples and as they went on their way many people would approach him. A young rich man came to Him seeking His counsel and a conversation ensued. Verses 17-22:

> 17 And when he was gone forth into the way, there came one running, and kneeled to him, and asked him, Good Master, what shall I do that I may inherit eternal life?
>
> 18 And Jesus said unto him, Why callest thou me good? there is none good but one, that is, God.
>
> 19 Thou knowest the commandments, Do not commit adultery, Do not kill, Do not steal, Do not bear false witness, Defraud not, Honour thy father and mother.
>
> 20 And he answered and said unto him, Master, all these have I observed from my youth.
>
> 21 Then Jesus beholding him loved him, and said unto him, One thing thou lackest: go thy way, sell whatsoever thou hast, and give to the poor, and thou

shalt have treasure in heaven: and come, take up the cross, and follow me.

22 And he was sad at that saying, and went away grieved: for he had great possessions.

Alone again with His disciples, Jesus explained that those who love material wealth are of the world. It will be difficult for them to enter the kingdom. Verses 23-27:

23 And Jesus looked round about, and saith unto his disciples, How hardly shall they that have riches enter into the kingdom of God!

24 And the disciples were astonished at his words. But Jesus answereth again, and saith unto them, Children, how hard is it for them that trust in riches to enter into the kingdom of God!

25 It is easier for a camel to go through the eye of a needle, than for a rich man to enter into the kingdom of God. 26 And they were astonished out of [beyond] measure, saying among themselves, Who then can be saved?

27 And Jesus looking upon them saith, With men it is impossible, but not with God: for with God all things are possible.

I picture them walking for a ways when Peter breaks the silence with a question. He was clearly thinking about what Jesus had said. Verses 28-31:

28 Then Peter began to say unto him, Lo, we have left all, and have followed thee.

29 And Jesus answered and said, Verily I say unto you, There is no man that hath left house, or brethren, or sisters, or father, or mother, or wife, or children, or lands, for my sake, and the gospel's,

30 But he shall receive an hundredfold now in this time, houses, and brethren, and sisters, and mothers, and children, and lands, with persecutions; and in the world to come eternal life.

31 But many that are first shall be last; and the last first.

This last verse requires some explanation. It has to do with believers who are alive at His Coming and those believers who are asleep. Believers who are alive at His Coming believed last, but they will be first. And, the believers who believed first will be resurrected to join the others. They will be last. We must keep our dispensations separate. Jesus came to confirm the promises made to the fathers. (See Romans 15:8.) The gospel preached by Jesus and the Twelve is the Gospel of the Kingdom. At this point in time, the Apostle Paul has not been sent yet. For a better understanding of the separate dispensations, I recommend two books. For beginners to intermediate Bible students, read *The Hidden Gospel: Once a Mystery But Now Revealed.* For the advanced Bible student, read *Letters To Theophilus: Are You Ready For The End Times?* These identify and explain the different ages or dispensations in the Word of Truth.

Jesus and His disciples are heading to Jerusalem. Verse 32:

> 32 **And they were in the way going up to Jerusalem; and Jesus went before them: and they were amazed; and as they followed, they were afraid. And he took again the twelve, and began to tell them what things should happen unto him,**

While along the way, Jesus took His disciples aside to explain what was going to take place. He did not want them to be surprised or to attempt to defend Him against His enemies. What will happen to Him must happen to fulfill all requirements. Verses 33-34:

> 33 Saying, Behold, we go up to Jerusalem; and the Son of man shall be delivered unto the chief priests, and unto the scribes; and they shall condemn him to death, and shall deliver him to the Gentiles:

> 34 And they shall mock him, and shall scourge him, and shall spit upon him, and shall kill him: and the third day he shall rise again.

Two of His disciples were brothers. They were known as the Sons of Thunder. Jesus gave them this nickname because of their passion and zeal. Sometimes, this led to them being aggressive or insensitive. Sensing that their time with Jesus was coming to an end, they boldly asked Him for a favor. Verses 35-41:

> 35 And James and John, the sons of Zebedee, come unto him, saying, Master, we would that thou shouldest do [grant] for us whatsoever we shall desire.

36 And he said unto them, What would ye that I should do for you?

37 They said unto him, Grant unto us that we may sit, one on thy right hand, and the other on thy left hand, in thy glory.

38 But Jesus said unto them, Ye know not what ye ask: can ye drink of the cup that I drink of? and be baptized with the baptism that I am baptized with?

39 And they said unto him, We can. And Jesus said unto them, Ye shall indeed drink of the cup that I drink of; and with the baptism that I am baptized withal shall ye be baptized:

40 But to sit on my right hand and on my left hand is not mine to give; but it shall be given to them for whom it is prepared.

41 And when the ten [others] heard it, they began to be much displeased with James and John.

Jesus stopped and called all the disciples together to prevent any division among them. Verses 42-45:

> 42 But Jesus called them to him, and saith unto them, Ye know that they which are accounted to rule over the Gentiles exercise lordship over them; and their great ones exercise authority upon them.

> 43 But so shall it not be among you: but whosoever will be great among you, shall be your minister: 44 And whosoever of you will be the chiefest, shall be servant of all.

> 45 For even the Son of man came not to be ministered unto, but to minister, and to give his life a ransom for many.

In the Gospel of Matthew, Jesus is called by the title "Son of David" ten times. We see it for the first time in the Gospel of Mark. It has to do with the Davidic Promise that God made to King David through Nathan the Prophet. 1 Chronicles 17:11-14:

> 11 And it shall come to pass, when thy days be expired that thou must go to be with thy fathers, that I will raise up thy

seed after thee, which shall be of thy sons; and I will establish his kingdom.

12 He shall build me an house, and I will stablish his throne for ever. 13 I will be his father, and he shall be my son: and I will not take my mercy away from him, as I took it from him [Saul] that was before thee:

14 But I will settle him in mine house and in my kingdom for ever: and his throne shall be established for evermore.

There is one more verse I would like you to see. At the beginning of the Gospel of Matthew, we find the geneaology of Jesus Christ. The very first verse of the New Testament establishes Jesus Christ as David's legitimate heir. Matthew 1:1:

1 The book of the generation of Jesus Christ, the son of David, the son of Abraham.

Along their journey to Jerusalem, they passed through Jericho. As Jesus was leaving the city a blind man wanted healing and called Him Son of David identifying Jesus as the future King. Mark 10:46-52:

46 And they came to Jericho: and as he went out of Jericho with his disciples and a great number of people, blind Bartimaeus, the son of Timaeus, sat by the highway side begging.

47 And when he heard that it was Jesus of Nazareth, he began to cry out, and say, Jesus, thou Son of David, have mercy on me.

48 And many charged him that he should hold his peace: but he cried the more a great deal, Thou Son of David, have mercy on me.

49 And Jesus stood still, and commanded him to be called. And they call the blind man, saying unto him, Be of good comfort, rise; he calleth thee.

50 And he, casting away his garment, rose, and came to Jesus. 51 And Jesus answered and said unto him, What wilt thou that I should do unto [for] thee? The blind man said unto him, Lord, that I might receive my sight.

52 And Jesus said unto him, Go thy way;

thy faith hath made thee whole. And immediately he received his sight, and followed Jesus in the way.

It is poetic that we find Jesus called Son of David. Jesus is the Son of God and the Son of David Who will be the eternal King of Israel. He is on His way to Jerusalem so that all the prophecies about Him will come true. Here is a prophecy written by Zechariah the Prophet concerning His entry into Jerusalem. Zechariah 9:9:

> 9 **Rejoice greatly, O daughter of Zion;**
> **shout, O daughter of Jerusalem:**
> **behold, thy King cometh unto thee:**
> **he is just, and having salvation;**
> **lowly, and riding upon an ass,**
> **and upon a colt the foal of an ass.**

At this point, it would be less than a week and He would be crucified. On the Cross upon which He will die, a sign written in three languages will be posted. Mark 15:26:

> 26 **And the superscription of his accusation was written over, THE KING OF THE JEWS.[!]**

12

Mark 11

Drawing near to Jerusalem, Jesus and the Twelve stopped. I picture them resting under the shade of trees and, here, he instructs them as to what must be done. Mark 11:1-7:

1 **And when they came nigh to Jerusalem, unto Bethphage and Bethany, at the mount of Olives, he sendeth forth two of his disciples,**

2 **And saith unto them, Go your way into the village over against you: and as soon as ye be entered into it, ye shall find a colt tied, whereon never man sat; loose him, and bring him.**

3 **And if any man say unto you, Why do ye this? say ye that the Lord hath need**

of him; and straightway he will send him hither.

4 And they went their way, and found the colt tied by the door without [outside] in a place where two ways met; and they loose [untie] him.

5 And certain of them that stood there said unto them, What do ye, loosing the colt? 6 And they said unto them even as Jesus had commanded: and they let them go.

7 And they brought the colt to Jesus, and cast their garments on him; and he sat upon him.

To follow is the record of Jesus' entry into Jerusalem as prophesied by Zechariah. Verses 8-10:

8 And many spread their garments in the way: and others cut down branches off the trees, and strawed them in the way.

9 And they that went before, and they that followed, cried, saying, <u>Hosanna;</u> <u>Blessed is he that cometh in the name of</u>

the Lord: 10 **Blessed be the kingdom of our father David, that cometh in the name of the Lord:** Hosanna in the highest.

The prophecy was well known by the Jews for they knew the Scriptures.

Jesus already knew what He would find in the Temple, but He wanted to see it with His own eyes. This Temple was dedicated to the glory of God and here He was standing there in the flesh. Verse 11:

11 **And Jesus entered into Jerusalem, and into the temple: and when he had looked round about upon all things, and now the eventide was come, he went out unto Bethany with the twelve.**

He would return to the Temple and deal with it later.

Bethany was the home of Mary, Martha, and Lazarus. It was only two miles from Jerusalem. He and the Twelve would rest there for the night. Verse 12:

12 **And on the morrow, when they were come from Bethany, he was hungry:**

The following is a figurative illustration made by Jesus. A landowner who leases out his land to tenants has certain expectations. The fig tree represents Israel. Verses 13-14:

> 13 And seeing a fig tree afar off having leaves, he came, if haply he might find any thing thereon: and when he came to it, he found nothing but leaves; for the time of figs was not yet.

> 14 And Jesus answered and said unto it, No man eat fruit of thee hereafter for ever. And his disciples heard it.

Jesus returned to the Temple and dealt with the corruption in the house of God. This is the first time we see Jesus angry. Verses 15-19:

> 15 And they come to Jerusalem: and Jesus went into the temple, and began to cast out them that sold and bought in the temple, and overthrew the tables of the moneychangers, and the seats of them that sold doves;

> 16 And would not suffer [allow] that any man should carry any vessel through the temple.

17 And he taught, saying unto them, Is it not written, My house shall be called of all nations the house of prayer? but ye have made it a den of thieves.

18 <u>And the scribes and chief priests heard it, and sought how they might destroy him</u>: for they feared him, because all the people was astonished at his doctrine.

19 And when even [evening] was come, he went out of the city.

I refer to this as Jesus knocking down a hornets' nest with the religious rulers being the hornets.

Returning to Jerusalem the next day, they passed the same fig tree. Verses 20-22:

20 And in the morning, as they passed by, they saw the fig tree dried up from the roots. 21 And Peter calling to remembrance saith unto him, Master, behold, the fig tree which thou cursedst is withered away.

22 And Jesus answering saith unto them, Have faith in God.

The disciples saw the state of the fig tree. Jesus tells them that they too, with faith, will have similar results. Verses 23-24:

> 23 **For verily I say unto you, That whoso-ever shall say unto this mountain, Be thou removed, and be thou cast into the sea; and shall not doubt in his heart, but shall believe that those things which he saith shall come to pass; he shall have whatsoever he saith.**

> 24 **Therefore I say unto you, What things soever ye desire, when ye pray, believe that ye receive them, and ye shall have them.**

It all has to do with having faith! When they ask God for something, they must believe that He hears them and will respond. It may not necessarily be with a "yes," but they must have faith that He will respond.

Jesus teaches His disciples something that applies to Kingdom Believers only. It makes forgiveness conditional and, therefore, it can only be applied to the Gospel of the Kingdom. Verses 25-26:

> 25 **And when ye stand praying, forgive, if ye have ought [anything] against any:**

that your Father also which is in heaven may forgive you your trespasses.
26 But if ye do not forgive, neither will your Father which is in heaven forgive your trespasses.

Forgiveness of their sins is dependent upon their forgiveness of the sins of others. We find this in the Lord's Prayer which is a model for Kingdom Believers. (See Matthew 6:9-13 and Luke 11:2-4.) In it, Jesus states, "And forgive us our debts, as we forgive our debtors" (Matt. 6:12). Those who follow the Gospel of Grace will clearly see the difference.

Arriving in Jerusalem, they enter the Temple where they are confronted by the religious leaders. Verses 27-28:

27 And they come again to Jerusalem: and as he was walking in the temple, there come to him the chief priests, and the scribes, and the elders,

28 And say unto him, By what authority doest thou these things? and who gave thee this authority to do these things?

Jesus responds to their question by asking them a question. Verses 29-33:

29 And Jesus answered and said unto them, I will also ask of you one question, and answer me, and I will tell you by what authority I do these things.

30 The baptism of John, was it from heaven, or of men? answer me.

31 And they reasoned with themselves, saying, If we shall say, From heaven; he will say, Why then did ye not believe him? 32 But if we shall say, Of men; they feared the people: for all men counted John, that he was a prophet indeed.

33 And they answered and said unto Jesus, We cannot tell. And Jesus answering saith unto them, Neither do I tell you by what authority I do these things.

13

Mark 12

Jesus did not answer the question posed by the religious leaders, but remained in the Temple. He begins to teach the people using parables. Mark 12:1-9:

1 **And he began to speak unto them by parables. A certain man planted a vineyard, and set an hedge about it, and digged a place for the winefat, and built a tower, and let it out to husbandmen, and went into a far country.**

2 **And at the season he sent to the husbandmen a servant, that he might receive from the husbandmen of the fruit of the vineyard.** 3 **And they caught him, and beat him, and sent him away empty.**

4 And again he sent unto them another servant; and at him they cast stones, and wounded him in the head, and sent him away shamefully handled.

5 And again he sent another; and him they killed, and many others; beating some, and killing some.

6 Having yet therefore one son, his well-beloved, he sent him also last unto them, saying, They will reverence my son.

7 But those husbandmen said among themselves, This is the heir; come, let us kill him, and the inheritance shall be ours. 8 And they took him, and killed him, and cast him out of the vineyard.

9 What shall therefore the lord of the vineyard do? he will come and destroy the husbandmen, and will give the vineyard unto others.

This is similar to the fig tree which Jesus cursed. It represents the religious leaders who were overseers to the nation of Israel. They had failed miserably at meeting the expectations of the Landowner.

The religious leaders did not leave, but stood there listening as Jesus taught the people. He quotes Psalms 118:22-23. Verses 10-12:

10 **And have ye not read this scripture; The stone which the builders rejected is become the head of the corner:**

11 **This was the Lord's doing, and it is marvellous in our eyes?**

12 **And they sought to lay hold on him, but feared the people: for they knew that he had spoken the parable against them: and they left him, and went their way.**

These learned men were intent on testing Jesus with their superior intellect. They desired to catch Him in an error and bring charges of blasphemy against Him. Verses 13-14:

13 **And they send unto him certain of the Pharisees and of the Herodians, to catch him in his words.**

14 **And when they were come, they say unto him, Master, we know that thou art true, and carest for no man: for thou re-**

gardest not the person of men, but teachest the way of God in truth: Is it lawful to give tribute to Caesar, or not?

Perhaps, He will speak words against Caesar and be guilty of treason. Verses 15-17:

15 Shall we give, or shall we not give? But he, knowing their hypocrisy, said unto them, Why tempt ye me? bring me a penny, that I may see it.

16 And they brought it. And he saith unto them, Whose is this image and superscription? And they said unto him, Caesar's.

17 And Jesus answering said unto them, Render to Caesar the things that are Caesar's, and to God the things that are God's. And they marvelled at him.

There were two groups of religious leaders who disagreed concerning the resurrection. The Pharisees believed in the resurrection, but the Sadducees did not. The latter wanted their chance to assail the future King also. Verses 18-23:

18 Then come unto him the Sadducees,

which say there is no resurrection; and they asked him, saying,

19 Master, Moses wrote unto us, If a man's brother die, and leave his wife behind him, and leave no children, that his brother should take his wife, and raise up seed unto his brother.

20 Now there were seven brethren: and the first took a wife, and dying left no seed. 21 And the second took her, and died, neither left he any seed: and the third likewise. 22 And the seven had her, and left no seed: last of all the woman died also.

23 In the resurrection therefore, when they shall rise, whose wife shall she be of them? for the seven had her to wife.

Did you catch the irony here? The Sadducees do not believe in the resurrection and yet it was the basis of their question.

Jesus responds to their question. Verses 24-27:

24 And Jesus answering said unto them, Do ye not therefore err, because ye

know not the scriptures, neither the power of God?

25 For when they shall rise from the dead, they neither marry, nor are given in marriage; but are as the angels which are in heaven.

26 And as touching [concerning] the dead, that they rise: have ye not read in the book of Moses, how in the bush God spake unto him, saying, I am the God of Abraham, and the God of Isaac, and the God of Jacob?

27 He is not the God of the dead, but the God of the living: ye therefore do greatly err.

One of the scribes was impressed with Jesus' answer. Being intrigued, he asked Him a sincere question. Verses 28-31:

28 And one of the scribes came, and having heard them reasoning together, and perceiving that he had answered them well, asked him, Which is the first commandment of all?

29 And Jesus answered him, The first of all the commandments is, <u>Hear, O Israel; The Lord our God is one Lord: 30 And thou shalt love the Lord thy God with all thy heart, and with all thy soul, and with all thy mind, and with all thy strength</u>: this is the first commandment.

31 And the second is like, namely this, <u>Thou shalt love thy neighbour as thyself</u>. There is none other commandment greater than these.

The scribe was genuinely pleased with the answer and agreed with it. Notice Jesus' response. Verses 32-34:

32 And the scribe said unto him, Well, Master, thou hast said the truth: for there is one God; and there is none other but he:

33 And to love him with all the heart, and with all the understanding, and with all the soul, and with all the strength, and to love his neighbour as himself, is more than all whole burnt offerings and sacrifices.

34 And when Jesus saw that he answered discreetly, he said unto him,
Thou art not far from the kingdom of
God. And no man after that durst
[dared] ask him any question.

This time, Jesus asked the scribes a question.
The people were there listening to this interaction
and He put them on the spot. We already looked at
the reason why Jesus could be called "the Son of David." Verses 35-37:

35 And Jesus answered and said, while
he taught in the temple, How say the
scribes that Christ [the Messiah] is the
Son of David?

36 For David himself said by the Holy
Ghost, The LORD said to my Lord, Sit
thou on my right hand, till I make thine
enemies thy footstool.

37 David therefore himself calleth him
Lord; and whence [how] is he then his
son? And the common people heard
him gladly.

The scribes were left speechless and the people were
pleased.

He took this opportunity to warn the people about false teachers. They do not teach the doctrines of God, but instead teach customs, traditions, and vain philosophies of men. Verses 38-40:

38 **And he said unto them in his doctrine, Beware of the scribes, which love to go in long clothing, and love salutations in the marketplaces,**

39 **And the chief seats in the synagogues, and the uppermost rooms at feasts:**

40 **Which devour widows' houses, and for a pretence make long prayers: these shall receive greater damnation.**

Jesus freely walked in the Temple and the courts surrounding it. He sat and observed as the people brought their tithes and offerings. He took this opportunity to teach His disciples about giving. Verses 41-44:

41 **And Jesus sat over against the treasury, and beheld how the people cast money into the treasury: and many that were rich cast in much.**

42 **And there came a certain poor widow,**

and she threw in two mites, which make a farthing.

43 And he called unto him his disciples, and saith unto them, Verily I say unto you, That this poor widow hath cast more in, than all they which have cast into the treasury:

44 For all they did cast in of their abundance; but she of her want did cast in all that she had, even all her living.

14

Mark 13

Upon leaving, a disciple looked at the beauty of the Temple and commented to Jesus about it. His response indicates that the glory of God will depart from the Temple. Forty years after His Crucifixion, the Temple will be completely destroyed. Mark 13:1-2:

> 1 And as he went out of the temple, one of his disciples saith unto him, Master, see what manner of stones and what buildings are here!

> 2 And Jesus answering said unto him, Seest thou these great buildings? there shall not be left one stone upon another, that shall not be thrown down.

Finding a place where they could sit, they asked

Jesus when this would happen and what would the signs be. We find a similar conversation to this one in Matthew 24. Verses 3-8:

3 And as he sat upon the mount of Olives over against the temple, Peter and James and John and Andrew asked him privately,

4 Tell us, when shall these things be? and what shall be the sign when all these things shall be fulfilled?

5 And Jesus answering them began to say, Take heed lest any man deceive you: 6 For many shall come in my name, saying, I am Christ; and shall deceive many.

7 And when ye shall hear of wars and rumours of wars, be ye not troubled: for such things must needs be; but the end shall not be yet. 8 For nation shall rise against nation, and kingdom against kingdom: and there shall be earthquakes in divers [different] places, and there shall be famines and troubles: these are the beginnings of sorrows.

The words "the beginnings of sorrows" refer to the start of the Tribulation. He lists what will happen at the beginning of the Tribulation which is also referred to as "the time of Jacob's trouble." Jacob and Israel are one in the same person. There will be seven years of testing of Israel and only "true" Israel will endure to the end. Look at the reference in Jeremiah 30:7:

> 7 Alas! for that day is great, so that none is like it: it is even the time of Jacob's trouble; but he shall be saved out of it.

Daniel's prophecy provided a 490-year timeline before the Kingdom will be established. The Messiah is cutoff after 483 years. This leaves only seven years remaining. The book *The Glorious Destiny of Israel: The Fulfillment of G-d's Promises and Promises to Israel.* It goes into great detail explaining this.

As we return to our text, Jesus is describing what will happen to Kingdom Believers during this time. Mark 13:9-13:

> 9 But take heed to yourselves: for they shall deliver you up to councils; and in the synagogues ye shall be beaten: and ye shall be brought before rulers and kings for my sake, for a testimony a-

gainst them. 10 And the gospel must first be published [preached] among all nations.

11 But when they shall lead you, and deliver you up, take no thought beforehand what ye shall speak, neither do ye premeditate: but whatsoever shall be given you in that hour, that speak ye: for it is not ye that speak, but the Holy Ghost.

12 Now the brother shall betray the brother to death, and the father the son; and children shall rise up against their parents, and shall cause them to be put to death.

13 And ye shall be hated of all men for my name's sake: but <u>he that shall endure unto the end, the same shall be saved.</u>

Jesus mentions the prophecy given to Daniel. Midway during the seven years, something terrible will happen. Following the Rapture, the Antichrist appears and signs a covenant. The Temple is rebuilt quickly and the sacrifices resume. Three and one-half years into the seven years, the Antichrist enters the

Temple and proclaims himself as god. The final three and one-half years are referred to as the "great tribulation."

It is this last half of the Tribulation to which Jesus is now referring. Verses 14-23:

> 14 But when ye shall see the abomination of desolation, spoken of by Daniel the prophet, standing where it ought not, (let him that readeth understand,) then let them that be in Judaea flee to the mountains:
>
> 15 And let him that is on the housetop not go down into the house, neither enter therein, to take any thing out of his house: 16 And let him that is in the field not turn back again for to take up his garment.
>
> 17 But woe to them that are with child, and to them that give suck in those days! 18 And pray ye that your flight be not in the winter. 19 For in those days shall be affliction, such as was not from the beginning of the creation which God created unto this time, neither shall be.

20 And except that the Lord had shortened those days, no flesh should be
saved: but for the elect's sake, whom he
hath chosen, he hath shortened the
days.

21 And then if any man shall say to you,
Lo, here is Christ; or, lo, he is there; believe him not: 22 For false Christs and
false prophets shall rise, and shall shew
signs and wonders, to seduce, if it were
possible, even the elect. 23 But take ye
heed: behold, I have foretold you all
things.

Jesus continues by describing what will happen at the conclusion of the seven years. We know
that there will be a great battle. This is the prelude to
the arrival of the King prepared for battle. Verses 24-
27:

24 But in those days, after that tribulation, the sun shall be darkened, and the
moon shall not give her light, 25 And the
stars of heaven shall fall, and the powers that are in heaven shall be shaken.

26 And then shall they see the Son of
man coming in the clouds with great

power and glory. 27 And then shall he send his angels, and shall gather together his elect from the four winds, from the uttermost part of the earth to the uttermost part of heaven.

Jesus reminds the Twelve of the fig tree. Verses 28-31:

28 Now learn a parable of the fig tree; When her branch is yet tender, and putteth forth leaves, ye know that summer is near:

29 So ye in like manner, when ye shall see these things come to pass, know that it is nigh [near], even at the doors.

30 Verily I say unto you, that <u>this generation shall not pass, till all these things be done</u> [completed].

31 Heaven and earth shall pass away: but my words shall not pass away.

Look at verse 29. Jesus is not speaking to the disciples about this "present" generation. Instead, He is talking about the generation who witness these signs. Whether it is seven years or two thousand years from then, the same generation who sees these things, they will see it completed. When they see these things happening, they will know that the end is near.

I like to say that the Rapture, in this present day, is imminent. It can occur at any time without warning. However, the Second Coming will happen at the end of the seven years. These seven years have a beginning, a middle, and an end. They begin at the arrival of the Antichrist who signs a covenant or treaty. The middle is marked by the abomination where the Antichrist declares in the Temple that he is god. (See Daniel 9.) The end is marked with signs of the times described above. These happen just before the Second Coming. The exact time is known by no one except the Father. Verse 32:

> 32 But of that day and that hour knoweth no man, no, not the angels which are in heaven, neither the Son, but the Father.

The following can only be a reference to Israel. The rulers of Israel were left to care for them until the arrival of the King. Israel must be watchful and ready to receive her King at His Coming. Verses 33-37:

> 33 Take ye heed, watch and pray: for ye know not when the time is. 34 For the Son of man is as a man taking a far jour-

ney, who left his house, and gave authority to his servants, and to every man his work, and commanded the porter to watch.

35 Watch ye therefore: for ye know not when the master of the house cometh, at even [evening], or at midnight, or at the cockcrowing, or in the morning:

36 Lest [at His] coming suddenly he find you sleeping. 37 And what I say unto you I say unto all, Watch.[!]

15

Mark 14 (Part I)

Treachery and deceit! First degree murder is premeditated. Here, the religious leaders are plotting to kill the Messiah. Consider again a parable Jesus told as recorded in the Gospel of Matthew. It is worth our time to repeat it here. Matthew 21:33-39:

> 33 Hear another parable: There was a certain householder, which planted a vineyard, and hedged it round about, and digged a winepress in it, and built a tower, and let it out to husbandmen, and went into a far country:

> 34 And when the time of the fruit drew near, he sent his servants to the husbandmen, that they might receive the fruits of it. 35 And the husbandmen took his servants, and beat one, and killed

another, and stoned another.

36 Again, he sent other servants more than the first: and they did unto them likewise.

37 But last of all he sent unto them his son, saying, They will reverence my son. 38 But when the husbandmen saw the son, they said among themselves, This is the heir; come, let us kill him, and let us seize on his inheritance.

39 And they caught him, and cast him out of the vineyard, and slew him.

Israel had killed the prophets whom God had sent to them. Now, they plotted to kill His Son. Mark 14:1-2:

1 After two days was the feast of the passover, and of unleavened bread: and the chief priests and the scribes sought how they might take him by craft, and put him to death. 2 But they said, Not on the feast day, lest there be an uproar of the people.

Jesus was dining with friends at a home in Bethany.

While He was there, a woman anointed His feet with an expensive oil. Verses 3-9:

> 3 And being in Bethany in the house of Simon the leper, as he sat at meat [a meal], there came a woman having an alabaster box of ointment of spikenard very precious; and she brake the box, and poured it on his head.

> 4 And there were some that had indignation within themselves [the disciples], and said, Why was this waste of the ointment made? 5 For it might have been sold for more than three hundred pence, and have been given to the poor. And they murmured against her.

> 6 And Jesus said, Let her alone; why trouble ye her? she hath wrought a good work on me. 7 For ye have the poor with you always, and whensoever ye will ye may do them good: but me ye have not always.

> 8 She hath done what she could: she is come aforehand [beforehand] to anoint my body to the burying.

9 Verily I say unto you, Wheresoever this gospel shall be preached throughout the whole world, this also that she hath done shall be spoken of for a memorial of her.

Judas left the Twelve to meet with the religious leaders. They made arrangements for the time and place to betray Jesus. Verse 10-11:

10 And Judas Iscariot, one of the twelve, went unto the chief priests, to betray him unto them. 11 And when they heard it, they were glad, and promised to give him money. And he sought how he might conveniently betray him.

The other disciples received instructions from Jesus to prepare a place for the Passover. Verses 12-16:

12 And the first day of unleavened bread, when they killed the passover [lamb], his disciples said unto him, Where wilt thou that we go and prepare that thou mayest eat the passover?

13 And he sendeth forth two of his disciples, and saith unto them, Go ye into the city, and there shall meet you a man

bearing a pitcher of water: follow him.

14 And wheresoever he shall go in, say ye to the goodman of the house, The Master saith, Where is the guestchamber, where I shall eat the passover with my disciples?

15 And he will shew you a large upper room furnished and prepared: there make ready for us.

16 And his disciples went forth, and came into the city, and found as he had said unto them: and they made ready the passover.

Finally, evening had come. Jesus looked forward to sharing this time with His disciples. Verses 17-21:

17 And in the evening he cometh with the twelve. 18 And as they sat and did eat, Jesus said, Verily I say unto you, One of you which eateth with me shall betray me.

19 And they began to be sorrowful, and to say unto him one by one, Is it I? and

another said, Is it I? 20 And he answered and said unto them, It is one of the twelve, that dippeth with me in the dish.

21 The Son of man indeed goeth, as it is written of him: but woe to that man by whom the Son of man is betrayed! good were it for that man if he had never been born.

Something that is very important will happen during the Last Supper. Verses 22-23:

22 And as they did eat, Jesus took bread, and blessed, and brake it, and gave to them, and said, Take, eat: this is my body. 23 And he took the cup, and when he had given thanks, he gave it to them: and they all drank of it.

The words "testament" and "covenant" are often used to mean the same. This is the case in the following verses. Jesus is referring to the fulfillment of an Old Testament prophecy. We will look at the prophecy concerning God making a new covenant with Israel and Judah. Not only does this describe the new covenant, but its fulfillment has to do with the future Kingdom. Jeremiah 31:31-33:

31 Behold, the days come, saith the LORD, that <u>I will make a new covenant with the house of Israel, and with the house of Judah</u>:

32 Not according to the covenant that I made with their fathers in the day that I took them by the hand to bring them out of the land of Egypt; which my covenant they brake, although I was an husband unto them, saith the LORD:

33 But this shall be the covenant that I will make with the house of Israel; After those days, saith the LORD, I will put my law in their inward parts, and write it in their hearts; and will be their God, and they shall be my people.

During the Passover, Jesus shared the bread and the cup. To this, He added the following statement. Mark 14:24-25:

24 And he said unto them, This is my blood of the new testament [covenant], which is shed for many. 25 Verily I say unto you, I will drink no more of the fruit of the vine, until that day that I drink it new in the kingdom of God.

No questions came from the disciples because what He said made sense. They were, no doubt, familiar with the prophecy. Now, they sang a hymn and departed. Verse 26:

> 26 **And when they had sung an hymn, they went out into the mount of Olives.**

Walking to the garden, Jesus spoke to them before the moment of His betrayal. He anticipated the arrival of those coming to arrest Him and He did not want them to be bewildered. Verses 27-28:

> 27 **And Jesus saith unto them, All ye shall be offended because of me this night: for it is written, I will smite the shepherd, and the sheep shall be scattered.**

> 28 **But after that I am risen, I will go before you into Galilee.**

Peter pledges his fidelity to Jesus and He responds. Verses 29-31:

> 29 **But Peter said unto him, Although all shall be offended, yet will not I.**

> 30 **And Jesus saith unto him, Verily I say**

unto thee, That this day, even in this night, before the cock crow twice, thou shalt deny me thrice.

31 But he [Peter] spake the more vehemently, If I should die with thee, I will not deny thee in any wise. Likewise also said they all.

The fidelity of all the disciples would soon be tested beyond their wildest imaginations.

We will continue with the remainder of Mark 14 in the next chapter.

16

Mark 14 (Part II)

Jesus and the Eleven arrived at the Garden of Gethsemane. There were only eleven because Judas was absent. Jesus desired to pray there alone. Mark 14:32-34:

> 32 **And they came to a place which was named Gethsemane: and he saith to his disciples, Sit ye here, while I shall pray.**
>
> 33 **And he taketh with him Peter and James and John, and began to be sore amazed, and to be very heavy; 34 And saith unto them, My soul is exceeding sorrowful unto death: tarry ye here, and watch.**

We must never forget the humanity of Christ. He is both fully-God and fully-man. He experiences the same emotions as we do. Pause for just a moment and consider what He was feeling? Jesus asked that His friends keep watch as He prayed. Verses 35-42:

35 And he went forward a little, and fell on the ground, and prayed that, if it were possible, the hour might pass from him. 36 And he said, Abba, Father, all things are possible unto thee; take away this cup from me: nevertheless not what I will, but what thou wilt.

37 And he cometh, and findeth them sleeping, and saith unto Peter, Simon, sleepest thou? couldest not thou watch one hour? 38 Watch ye and pray, lest ye enter into temptation. The spirit truly is ready, but the flesh is weak.

39 And again he went away, and prayed, and spake the same words. 40 And when he returned, he found them asleep again, (for their eyes were heavy,) neither wist [knew] they what to answer him.

41 And he cometh the third time, and saith unto them, Sleep on now, and take your rest: it is enough, the hour is come;

behold, the Son of man is betrayed into the hands of sinners.

42 Rise up, let us go; lo, he that betrayeth me is at hand.

A large crowd came to capture Him as if He was a violent criminal. They were armed and, no doubt, expecting resistance. Instead, like a lamb He would be led away by His captives. Do you recall the words used in Daniel's prophecy? "Shall Messiah be cut off" (Dan. 9:26). This fulfills another prophecy as well. Isaiah 53:7-8:

> **7 He was oppressed, and he was afflicted, yet he opened not his mouth: he is brought as a lamb to the slaughter, and as a sheep before her shearers is dumb, so he openeth not his mouth.**
>
> **8 He was taken from prison and from judgment: and who shall declare his generation? for he was cut off out of the land of the living:**

We return to our text at the point where Judas arrives to greet his Master. Mark 14:43-45:

43 And immediately, while he yet spake,

cometh Judas, one of the twelve, and with him a great multitude with swords and staves, from the chief priests and the scribes and the elders.

44 And he that betrayed him had given them a token, saying, Whomsoever I shall kiss, that same is he; take him, and lead him away safely. 45 And as soon as he was come, he goeth straightway to him, and saith, Master, master; and kissed him.

This kiss was to identify the One Who was the Christ. It was the kiss of betrayal!

There was a confrontation between this mob and the disciples who stood with Him. Verses 46-47:

46 And they laid their hands on him, and took him. 47 And one of them [the disciples] that stood by drew a sword, and smote a servant of the high priest, and cut off his ear.

This is precisely what Jesus sought to avoid. One of His disciples acted by cutting off the ear of a servant. The Gospel of Luke tells us that Jesus healed the servant's ear. Luke 22:50-51:

50 And one of them smote the servant of the high priest, and cut off his right ear. 51 And Jesus answered and said, Suffer ye thus far. And he touched his ear, and healed him.

We return to our text. Mark 14:48-49:

48 And Jesus answered and said unto them, Are ye come out, as against a thief, with swords and with staves to take me?

49 I was daily with you in the temple teaching, and ye took me not: but the scriptures must be fulfilled.

At this point, all of Jesus' disciples fled along with those who followed Him so that He was alone. Verses 50-52:

50 And they all forsook him, and fled. 51 And there followed him a certain young man, having a linen cloth cast about his naked body; and the young men laid hold on him:

52 And he left the linen cloth, and fled from them naked.

They led Jesus way and brought Him to the conclave of religious leaders waiting for His arraignment. Verse 53:

> 53 **And they led Jesus away to the high priest: and with him were assembled all the chief priests and the elders and the scribes.**

All had forsaken Jesus, but Peter remained not far from Him watching. Verse 54:

> 54 **And Peter followed him afar off, even into the palace of the high priest: and he sat with the servants, and warmed himself at the fire.**

Inside, they were looking to charge Jesus with the religious crime of blasphemy so that they could condemn Him to death. Verses 55-65:

> 55 **And the chief priests and all the council sought for witness against Jesus to put him to death; and found none.** 56 **For many bare false witness against him, but their witness agreed not together.**

> 57 **And there arose certain, and bare false witness against him, saying,**

58 We heard him say, I will destroy this temple that is made with hands, and within three days I will build another made without hands.

59 But neither so did their witness agree together. 60 And the high priest stood up in the midst, and asked Jesus, saying, Answerest thou nothing? what is it which these witness against thee?

61 But he held his peace [remained silent], and answered nothing. Again the high priest asked him, and said unto him, Art thou the Christ, the Son of the Blessed?

62 And Jesus said, I am: and ye shall see the Son of man sitting on the right hand of power, and coming in the clouds of heaven. 63 Then the high priest rent his clothes, and saith, What need we any further witnesses?

64 <u>Ye have heard the blasphemy</u>: what think ye? <u>And they all condemned him to be guilty of death.</u>

65 And some began to spit on him, and

to cover his face, and to buffet him, and to say unto him, Prophesy: and the servants did strike him with the palms of their hands.

Outside the hearing, Peter stood warming himself beside a fire with others. Verses 66-72:

66 And as Peter was beneath in the palace, there cometh one of the maids of the high priest:

67 And when she saw Peter warming himself, she looked upon him, and said, And thou also wast with Jesus of Nazareth. 68 But he denied, saying, I know not, neither understand I what thou sayest. And he went out into the porch; and the cock crew.

69 And a maid saw him again, and began to say to them that stood by, This is one of them. 70 And he denied it again. And a little after, they that stood by said again to Peter, Surely thou art one of them: for thou art a Galilaean, and thy speech agreeth thereto.

71 But he began to curse and to swear,

saying, I know not this man of whom ye speak.

72 And the second time the cock crew. And Peter called to mind [remembered] the word that Jesus said unto him, Before the cock crow twice, thou shalt deny me thrice. And when he thought thereon, he wept.

17

Mark 15

The religious leaders of Israel had unanimously determined that Jesus was guilty of blasphemy and worthy of death. Mark 15:1:

1 And straightway in the morning the chief priests held a consultation with the elders and scribes and the whole council, and bound Jesus, and carried him away, and delivered him to Pilate.

Pontius Pilate held the title of Prefect or Governor over the province of Judaea. His authority was granted to him by the Roman Emperor and he administrated Roman Law in that region. For that reason, Jesus was brought before him for His trial. Verses 2-5:

2 And Pilate asked him [Jesus], Art thou

> the King of the Jews? And he answering
> said unto him, Thou sayest it. 3 And the
> chief priests accused him of many
> things: but he answered nothing.
>
> 4 And Pilate asked him again, saying,
> Answerest thou nothing? behold how
> many things they witness against thee.
> 5 But Jesus yet answered nothing; so
> that Pilate marvelled.

Do you remember the prophecy? "He was op-
pressed, and he was afflicted, yet he opened not his
mouth" (Isa. 53:7).

Passover was one of the most important feasts
of the year. It was a custom that the Governor would
release one criminal at the choice of the people.
Verses 6-7:

> 6 Now at that feast he released unto
> them one prisoner, whomsoever they
> desired. 7 And there was one named
> Barabbas, which lay bound with them
> that had made insurrection with him,
> who had committed murder in the in-
> surrection.

Their choice was between a convicted murderer and

the One called "the King of the Jews."

Like most crowds, they were easily influenced by the religious leaders. Verses 8-16:

8 And the multitude crying aloud began to desire him to do as he had ever done unto them.

9 But Pilate answered them, saying, Will ye that I release unto you the King of the Jews? 10 For he knew that the chief priests had delivered him for envy.

11 But the chief priests moved the people, that he should rather release Barabbas unto them. 12 And Pilate answered and said again unto them, What will ye then that I shall do unto him whom ye call the King of the Jews?

13 And they cried out again, Crucify him. 14 Then Pilate said unto them, Why, what evil hath he done? And they cried out the more exceedingly, Crucify him.

15 And so Pilate, willing to content [appease] the people, released Barabbas

unto them, and delivered Jesus, when he had scourged him, to be crucified.

16 And the soldiers led him away into the hall, called Praetorium; and they call together the whole band.

This was like throwing Jesus to the wolves. It was customary that part of any prisoner's punishment included the mistreatment by the soldiers. As He was brought into the garrison area, they called to their friends to join in tormenting the accused. Verses 17-25:

17 And they clothed him with purple, and platted a crown of thorns, and put it about his head, 18 And began to salute him, Hail, King of the Jews!

19 And they smote him on the head with a reed, and did spit upon him, and bowing their knees worshipped him. 20 And when they had mocked him, they took off the purple from him, and put his own clothes on him, and led him out to crucify him.

21 And they compel [forced] one Simon a Cyrenian, who passed by, coming out

162

of the country, the father of Alexander and Rufus, to bear his cross.

22 And they bring him unto the place Golgotha, which is, being interpreted, The place of a skull. 23 And they gave him to drink wine mingled with myrrh: but he received it not.

24 And when they had crucified him, they parted his garments, casting lots upon them, what every man should take.

25 And it was the third hour, and they crucified him.

It was still early morning. The third hour would be nine o'clock.

The crime Jesus committed was posted at the top of the Cross for all to see. According to the Gospel of Luke, it was ". . . written over him in letters of Greek, and Latin, and Hebrew . . ." (Lk. 23:38). Our text continues. Verses 26-32:

26 And the superscription of his accusation was written over, THE KING OF THE JEWS.

27 And with him they crucify two thieves; the one on his right hand, and the other on his left. 28 And the scripture was fulfilled, which saith, And he was numbered with the transgressors.

29 And they that passed by railed on him, wagging their heads, and saying, Ah, thou that destroyest the temple, and buildest it in three days, 30 Save thyself, and come down from the cross.

31 Likewise also the chief priests mocking said among themselves with the scribes, He saved others; himself he cannot save. 32 Let Christ the King of Israel descend now from the cross, that we may see and believe. And they that were crucified with him reviled him.

Jesus had hung on the Cross for three hours by noontime. At that point, the skies became dark like night and remained that way until three o'clock. Verse 33:

33 And when the sixth hour was come, there was darkness over the whole land until the ninth hour.

Then, about three o'clock, Jesus spoke. Verse 34:

> 34 And at the ninth hour Jesus cried with a loud voice, saying, Eloi, Eloi, lama sabachthani? which is, being interpreted, My God, my God, why hast thou forsaken me?

John the Baptist proclaimed at the beginning of Jesus' ministry, " . . . Behold the Lamb of God!" (Jn. 1:36). Jesus was the Passover Lamb. He was taking upon Himself the sins of the world. God, being perfect, could not look upon sin. For that reason, Jesus felt abandoned by His Father.

A crowd stood and watched the executions. They wanted to see what Jesus would do. Verses 35-38:

> 35 And some of them that stood by, when they heard it, said, Behold, he calleth Elias.

> 36 And one ran and filled a spunge full of vinegar, and put it on a reed, and gave him to drink, saying, Let alone; let us see whether Elias will come to take him down.

37 And Jesus cried with a loud voice, and gave up the ghost. **38** And the veil of the temple was rent in twain from the top to the bottom.

Jesus cried in anguish and died. Symbolically, the Temple curtain was cut in two from top to bottom.

There were those who stood near Him who heard Him speak. Even the centurion recognized the supernatural aspects of His crucifixion. Verse 39:

39 And when the centurion, which stood over against [opposite to] him, saw that he so cried out, and gave up the ghost, he said, Truly this man was the Son of God.

At a distance away from the gruesome scene, there were the women who were in Jesus' life. Many of them had been with Him throughout His ministry. Verses 40-41:

40 There were also women looking on afar off: among whom was Mary Magdalene, and Mary the mother of James the less and of Joses, and Salome;

41 (Who also, when he was in Galilee,

followed him, and ministered unto him;) and many other women which came up with him unto Jerusalem.

The women were concerned for His body. God provides. A man of good reputation took it upon himself to speak with Pontius Pilate and offered an appropriate burial place. Verses 42-45:

> **42 And now when the even [evening] was come, because it was the preparation, that is, the day before the sabbath,**

> **43 Joseph of Arimathaea, an honourable counsellor, which also waited for the kingdom of God, came, and went in boldly unto Pilate, and craved the body of Jesus.**

> **44 And Pilate marvelled if he were already dead: and calling unto him the centurion, he asked him whether he had been any while dead. 45 And when he knew it of the centurion, he gave the body to Joseph.**

Joseph of Arimathaea owned a burial tomb. They removed His body from the Cross in the twilight and quickly wrapped it in linen. Since it was already evening, the women would return later to finish after the Sabbath.

The crowd had dispersed and a quiet peace settled over the place. They made their hurried preparation because the Sabbath begins on the evening before at sunset. Verses 46-47:

46 **And he bought fine linen, and took him down, and wrapped him in the linen, and laid him in a sepulchre which was hewn out of a rock, and rolled a stone unto the door of the sepulchre.**

47 **And Mary Magdalene and Mary the mother of Joses beheld where he was laid.**

The large stone was rolled across its doorway. The powers, principalities, and rulers of darkness rejoiced over their victory, but the heavenly host mourned the death of the only Son of God.

18

Mark 16

God created the heavens and the earth in six days. He rested on the seventh day. Israel was told to honor the Sabbath and keep it holy from all other days. So, the women returned to the tomb at sunrise the day after the Sabbath. Mark 16:1-6:

1 **And when the sabbath was past, Mary Magdalene, and Mary the mother of James, and Salome, had bought sweet spices, that they might come and anoint him.** 2 **And very early in the morning the first day of the week, they came unto the sepulchre at the rising of the sun.**

3 **And they said among themselves, Who shall roll us away the stone from the door of the sepulchre?** 4 **And when they looked, they saw that the stone was**

rolled away: for it was very great.

5 And entering into the sepulchre, they saw a young man sitting on the right side, clothed in a long white garment; and they were affrighted.

6 And he saith unto them, Be not affrighted: Ye seek Jesus of Nazareth, which was crucified: he is risen; he is not here: behold the place where they laid him.

I can picture the angel motioning with his hand to where the body had laid. He instructs the women to go and tell the others that He has risen! Verses 7-8:

7 But go your way, tell his disciples and Peter that he goeth before you into Galilee: there shall ye see him, as he said unto you.

8 And they went out quickly, and fled from the sepulchre; for they trembled and were amazed: neither said they any thing to any man; for they were afraid.

The resurrected Lord appears to Mary Magdalene. She went to the disciples and told them, but they did not believe her. Verses 9-11:

> 9 Now when Jesus was risen early the first day of the week, he appeared first to Mary Magdalene, out of whom he had cast seven devils [demons].

> 10 And she went and told them that had been with him, as they mourned and wept. 11 And they, when they had heard that he was alive, and had been seen of her, believed not.

Again, He appeared to others as they walked along a way and, when they told others, they did not believe. Verses 12-13:

> 12 After that he appeared in another form unto two of them, as they walked, and went into the country. 13 And they went and told it unto the residue [others]: neither believed they them.

Then, Jesus appeared to the disciples as they sat at a meal. He rebuked them. Verse 14:

> 14 Afterward he appeared unto the eleven as they sat at meat, and upbraided them with their unbelief and

hardness of heart, because they believed not them which had seen him after he was risen.

He instructs them about their mission. Verses 15-16:

15 And he said unto them, Go ye into all the world, and preach the gospel to every creature. 16 He that believeth and is baptized shall be saved; but he that believeth not shall be damned.

The disciples knew the message of the Gospel of the Kingdom. At this point, the Tribulation was imminent and only seven years remained until the Kingdom would be established.

The Jews require miracles, signs, and wonders as God's authentication. Jesus tells them what signs they can expect. Verses 17-18:

17 And these signs shall follow them that believe; In my name shall they cast out devils; they shall speak with new tongues;

18 They shall take up serpents; and if they drink any deadly thing, it shall not

hurt them; they shall lay hands on the sick, and they shall recover.

In other books, I discuss the unique nature of the word "and" as being a possible time indicator. An example I use is, "She was born in London and died in Boston. The point is that there can be a span of time indicated by the conjunction "and." The Gospel of Mark is the shortest of the three synoptic gospels having only sixteen chapters. The Gospel of Matthew has twenty-eight and the Gospel of Luke has twenty-four chapters.

Let us look at the additional details provided by these two other gospels. Matthew 28:16-20:

> **16 Then the eleven disciples went away into Galilee, into a mountain where Jesus had appointed them. 17 And when they saw him, they worshipped him: but some doubted. 18 And Jesus came and spake unto them, saying, All power is given unto me in heaven and in earth.**
>
> **19 Go ye therefore, and teach all nations, baptizing them in the name of the Father, and of the Son, and of the Holy Ghost: 20 Teaching them to observe all things whatsoever I have commanded**

you: and, lo, I am with you alway, even unto the end of the world. Amen.

Remember, Jesus is speaking to His eleven disciples who are Jewish. These are not marching orders for the present-day church. It is the same gospel which Jesus told the Twelve to take to "the lost sheep of the house of Israel" and not to the Gentiles! Look that Jesus' instructions to the Twelve in Matthew 10:5-7:

> 5 **These twelve Jesus sent forth, and commanded them, saying, <u>Go not into the way of the Gentiles</u>, and into any city of the Samaritans enter ye not:**
>
> 6 **<u>But go rather to the lost sheep of the house of Israel</u>. 7 And as ye <u>go, preach, saying, The kingdom of heaven is at hand</u>.**

The Gospel of the Kingdom has to do with the coming Kingdom.

As we come to the end of the Gospel of Mark, it is important you notice something. The Gospel of the Kingdom requires that the Kingdom Believers be taught "to observe all things whatsoever I have commanded you" (Matt. 28:20). These believers are still under the requirements of the Law of Moses. They

174

are in the Age of Law! The Age of Grace will not be introduced until the conversion of the Apostle Paul. Jesus gave His instructions to the eleven disciples who were unaware of any other gospel than the Gospel of the Kingdom.

Now, let us turn to the Gospel of Luke to compare the conclusion of his gospel account. Luke 24:44-50:

> 44 And he said unto them, These are the words which I spake unto you, while I was yet with you, that <u>all things must be fulfilled, which were written in the law of Moses, and in the prophets, and in the psalms</u>, concerning me.
>
> 45 Then opened he their understanding, that they might understand the scriptures, 46 And said unto them, Thus it is written, and thus it behoved Christ to suffer, and to rise from the dead the third day:
>
> 47 <u>And that repentance and remission of sins should be preached in his name among all nations, beginning at Jerusalem.</u> 48 And ye are witnesses of these things.

49 And, behold, I send the promise of my Father upon you: but tarry ye in the city of Jerusalem, until ye be endued with power from on high.

50 And he led them out as far as to Bethany, and he lifted up his hands, and blessed them.

Luke includes Jesus' promise of the Holy Spirit Who would come at Pentecost. Then, he records the Ascension. Verses 51-53:

51 And it came to pass, while he blessed them, <u>he was parted from them, and carried up into heaven.</u>

52 And they worshipped him, and returned to Jerusalem with great joy: **53** And were continually in the temple, praising and blessing God.

Let us see how the Gospel of Mark ends. Mark ends with only a statement of Jesus' Ascension to conclude His gospel account. Mark 16:19:

19 So then after the Lord had spoken unto them, he was received up into heaven, and sat on the right hand of

God.

Notice that Jesus is presently seated at the right hand of God where He will remain until something is completed. King David recorded God the Father speaking to God the Son. Psalms 110:1:

> 1 **The LORD said unto my Lord, <u>Sit thou at my right hand, until I make thine enemies thy footstool.</u>**

To gain a deeper understanding of Israel's destiny and future, consider reading *The Glorious Destiny of Israel: The Fulfillment of G-d's Promises and Promises to Israel.*

The following brings us to the conclusion of the Gospel of Mark. Mark 16:20:

> 20 **And they [the disciples] went forth, and preached every where, the Lord working with them, and confirming the word with signs following. Amen.**

Epilogue

At the end of a book, I like to provide some closing comments to highlight important points I would like to make. When we approach the Bible dispensationally, it is important not to hop or straddle fences. The danger comes when we try to assimilate two different dispensations into one. I made this point in the Introduction. When we do not understand right division, the interpretation of the Word of Truth may focus on what the message is, but not to whom that message is sent.

Jesus came to the children of Abraham, Isaac, and Jacob. God made promises and prophecies in the Old Testament that belong to Israel. Later, Paul would explain to the Gentiles the purpose of Jesus' earthly ministry. Repetition, on such a key point, is necessary. Romans 15:8

> 8 Now I say that <u>Jesus Christ was a minister of the circumcision</u> for the truth of God, <u>to confirm the promises made un-</u>

to the fathers:

The word "confirm" means "to establish the certainty" of something. Paul applied this specifically to God's promise to King David concerning his everlasting throne. That promise concerns God establishing the eternal kingdom with His Son, Jesus Christ, as the eternal King. For that reason, the Gospel of the Kingdom, delivered to the lost sheep of the house of Israel, "confirms" this coming Kingdom.

In my opinion, the majority of evangelical churches today preach the Gospel of the Kingdom. You may hear their clergy use words like "for the furtherance of the kingdom" or "to build the kingdom." Many preachers try to merge the Gospel of the Kingdom with the Gospel of Grace, but Paul says that doing so makes it not a gospel at all. (See Galatians 1:6-9.)

Let us make sure that you aware that there are two distinct gospels. This is not taught or known in most churches or assemblies today. It is as simple as the following example. Bobby would take the red bike and Dave would take the blue bike. How many bikes are there in the previous sentence? The answer is simple. Are there not two bikes? Now, let us apply this to the verses from Galatan 2. When we read the first two chapters of Galatians, we find that, later on, there was a meeting between the Kingdom Apostles and the Apostle Paul. At this meeting they reached a mutual agreement. Galatians 2:7-9:

> 7 But contrariwise, when they saw that <u>the gospel of the uncircumcision</u> was committed unto me [Paul], as <u>the gospel of the circumcision</u> was unto Peter;
>
> 8 (For he that wrought effectually in Peter to the apostleship of the circumcision, the same was mighty in me toward the Gentiles:)
>
> 9 And when James, Cephas [Peter], and John, who seemed to be pillars, perceived the grace that was given unto me, they gave to me and Barnabas the right hands of fellowship; <u>that we should go unto the heathen, and they unto the circumcision.</u>

We know that the Jews are called the "circumcision" because of the sign of the Abrahamic Covenant. Gentiles are the "uncircumcision" and aliens from the commonwealth of Israel. Ephesians 2:11-12:

> 11 Wherefore remember, that ye being in

time past <u>Gentiles in the flesh, who are called Uncircumcision</u> by that which is called the Circumcision in the flesh made by hands;

12 That at that time ye were without Christ, being aliens from the commonwealth of Israel, and strangers from the covenants of promise, having no hope, and without God in the world.

The above information was presented again for one purpose alone. I wanted to make sure you know that there are two gospels in the New Testament. I confess that I desired to write a summary here of the two gospels. However, without laying out details including the context, history, and dispensational boundaries, I would be doing both you and the gospel messages a disservice. The best I can do is make you aware of the two gospels and leave you to study them further.

As a teacher, I would be foolish to try and fit all the material of a semester into one class. The same concept applies to the two gospels. The following reading suggestions to you are not self-serving. I recommend them because I know their content and presentation. Therefore, I can confidently recommend *The Hidden Gospel: Once Hidden But Now Re-*

vealed. It is a summary of the Bible from Genesis to Revelation. It lays out all of the dispensations as well as explaining them and their purpose. This book is for the beginner to intermediate Bible student.

There are two more books I recommend. Both are for the more advanced Bible student interested in gaining a deeper understanding of God's Word. The first is *Letters To Theophilus: Are You Ready For The End Times?* This book, like the one above, is a summary of the Bible. It is seen from the Gentile's perspective. It includes information about Israel and includes the Gospel of Grace.

The other book is *The Glorious Destiny of Israel: The Fulfillment of G-d's Promises and Prophecies to Israel.* This book is dedicated to the children of Abraham. As such, it focuses exclusively on the promises and prophecies that God gave to Israel. It looks at the Bible from a dispensational perspective as it applies to Israel. The book does not try to convert the children of Abraham from the Gospel of the Kingdom, but directs those who are interested in understanding the Gospel of Grace to *Letters To Theophilus.* This book is very popular with Messianic Jews.

Other GraceWord Publications

In English:

1st Corinthians: Dispensationally Considered
1st & 2nd Thessalonians: Dispensationally Con.
1st & 2nd Timothy & Titus: Dispensationally Con.
2nd Corinthians: Dispensationally Considered
Acts: Dispensationally Considered
Colossians & Philemon: Dispensationally Con.
Ephesians: Dispensationally Considered
Galatians: Dispensationally Considered
Hebrews: Dispensationally Considered
How Am I Wired?
Letters To Theophilus
Philippians: Dispensationally Considered
Romans: Dispensationally Considered
The Glorious Destiny Of Israel
The Gospel of John: Dispensationally Con.
The Gospel of Luke: Dispensationally Con.
The Gospel of Matthew: Dispensationally Con.
The Hidden Gospel
The Seven Hebrew Epistles: Dispensationally Con.

Two Distinct Gospel Messages Of The New Test.

En español:

Cartas A Teófilo
Efesios: Dispensacionalmente considerado
El evangelio Oculto: Una vest fue un misterio . . .

About The Author

Dr. David Alan Greene has over thirty-five years of experience as an insurance agent selling both property and casualty as well as life insurance. During his career, he taught and explained the content and meaning of policies to his clients. Now retired, he devotes much of his time to teaching the Bible.

He obtained his Bachelor of Theology, Master of Biblical Studies, and Ph.D. in Biblical Studies from Evangelical Theological Seminary where he holds the position of Dean of Graduate Studies. He also holds a Ph.D. in Christian Counseling. He has written numerous biblical commentaries and books on rightly dividing the Word of Truth.

9 798998 531330